ARROYO CENTER

T0302882

Toward Operational Art in Special Warfare

Dan Madden, Dick Hoffmann, Michael Johnson, Fred T. Krawchuk,
Bruce R. Nardulli, John E. Peters, Linda Robinson, Abby Doll

Prepared for the United States Army

For more information on this publication, visit www.rand.org/t/rr779

Library of Congress Control Number: 2016932113
ISBN: 978-0-8330-8763-8

Published by the RAND Corporation, Santa Monica, Calif.
© Copyright 2016 RAND Corporation
RAND® is a registered trademark.

Support RAND

Make a tax-deductible charitable contribution at
www.rand.org/giving/contribute

www.rand.org

Preface

This report demonstrates the need for a strategic and operational approach to securing U.S. interests called *special warfare*. The United States requires new approaches for exerting influence, filling the missing middle between the limitations of distant-strike options presented by armed unmanned aerial systems and Tomahawk missiles and the costly, indefinite commitment of conventional forces.

Special warfare is an Army Special Operations Forces doctrinal term meaning the "execution of activities that involve a combination of lethal and nonlethal actions taken by a specially trained and educated force that has a deep understanding of cultures and foreign language, proficiency in small-unit tactics, and the ability to build and fight alongside indigenous combat formations in a permissive, uncertain, or hostile environment." It includes "special operations forces conducting combinations of unconventional warfare, foreign internal defense, and/or counterinsurgency through and with indigenous forces or personnel."[1]

The report has four aims: (1) to adapt conventional operational art to the unique characteristics of special warfare, (2) to identify the strategic advantages and risks associated with special warfare, (3) to explore how special warfare campaigns could be used to address challenges identified in strategic guidance, and (4) to provide guidance to military and civilian leaders and planners in designing and executing these campaigns.

---

[1] Headquarters, U.S. Department of the Army, *Special Operations*, Army Doctrine Publication 3-05, Washington, D.C., August 2012c, p. 9.

The second volume of this report, *Toward Operational Art in Special Warfare: Appendixes* (available online at www.rand.org/t/RR779), offers additional context to supplement the discussions presented here. Appendix A in that volume provides a brief overview of the evolution of operational art. Appendix B summarizes the literature on developing consensus among groups or individuals with disparate goals and approaches and explains how this could be used in special warfare planning. Appendix C reviews the resources and authorities for special warfare. Appendix D provides additional details on our data set of special warfare campaigns conducted by the United States since World War II. Appendix E presents notional special warfare campaigns that could be used to train special warfare campaign planners and assist the U.S. Department of Defense in identifying capability requirements for special warfare campaigns. Appendix F explores in greater depth the special operations activity "preparation of the environment." Finally, Appendix G offers a detailed discussion of the recommendations presented in Chapter Six of this report.

This research was sponsored by LTG Charles T. Cleveland, then commanding general of U.S. Army Special Operations Command, and conducted within the RAND Arroyo Center's Strategy, Doctrine, and Resources Program. RAND Arroyo Center, part of the RAND Corporation, is a federally funded research and development center sponsored by the United States Army.

The Project Unique Identification Code (PUIC) for the project that produced this document is RAN136470.

Contents

Figures and Tables

Figures

Tables

Summary

In the face of adversaries exploiting regional social cleavages through the use of special operations forces (SOF) and intelligence services, coupled with a dwindling appetite for intervention, the United States needs to employ a more sophisticated form of special warfare to secure its interests.[1] Special warfare campaigns stabilize a friendly state or destabilize a hostile regime by operating "through and with" local state or nonstate partners, rather than through unilateral U.S. action. SOF are the primary U.S. military forces employed, but successful campaigns depend on a broad suite of joint and U.S. government capabilities. Special warfare has particular relevance to the current global security environment as policymakers seek options short of large-scale intervention to manage (or assist in managing) challenges both acute (e.g., Syrian civil war, Ukraine crisis) and chronic (e.g., insurgency in the Philippines).

Special warfare fills the missing middle for exerting influence between precision-strike options provided by armed unmanned aerial systems, SOF raids, aircraft and missiles, and the costly commitment of conventional forces. The potential for escalation associated with precision-strike capabilities may render them too risky to employ in some circumstances.[2] In cases in which the targeted regime's core inter-

---

[1] Headquarters, U.S. Department of the Army, *Special Operations*, Army Doctrine Publication 3-05, Washington, D.C., August 2012c, p. 9; U.S. Joint Chiefs of Staff, *Special Operations*, Joint Publication 3-05, Washington, D.C., July 16, 2014, p. xi.

[2] David Gompert and Terrence Kelly, "Escalation Cause: How the Pentagon's New Strategy Could Trigger War with China," *Foreign Policy*, August 2, 2013.

ests are involved, precision-strike options may be insufficient to compel desired changes in behavior.[3]

Despite policymaker antipathy toward the costs and risks of intervention, observed and forecasted instability around the world will continue to create situations in which policymakers are forced to act to protect U.S. interests.[4] Special warfare provides policymakers with an additional option that can help achieve interests and manage risks in some important cases.

Special warfare is not new. The United States has a long (and somewhat checkered) history of special warfare operations. Classic cases from the 1980s include U.S. support to the government of El Salvador against the Farabundo Martí National Liberation Front (FMLN) Marxist insurgents and to the Mujahedeen in Afghanistan against the Soviets. In the former case, the U.S. military was restricted to providing no more than 55 advisers, who did not participate in combat operations. In the latter case, operations were conducted almost entirely from and through a third country, Pakistan.[5] Today, operations in Colombia and the Philippines constitute classic cases of special warfare. However, more than a decade of focus on Iraq, Afghanistan, and global counterterrorism has atrophied U.S. special warfare campaign design skills in the military and appreciation for special warfare's employment as a strategic tool in the policy community. This report provides an intellectual framework for integrating the planning efforts of special operations and conventional forces, the combatant commands, the U.S. Department of State (DoS), the intelligence community, and policymakers.

The United States is not the only country with special warfare capabilities. Russia has recently been successful in exploiting a

---

[3]   Ivo Daalder and Michael O'Hanlon, *Winning Ugly: NATO's War to Save Kosovo*, Washington, D.C.: Brookings Institution Press, 2000.

[4]   National Intelligence Council, *Global Trends 2030: Alternative Worlds*, Washington, D.C., 2012.

[5]   Steve Coll, *Ghost Wars: The Secret History of the CIA, Afghanistan, and bin Laden, from the Soviet Invasion to September 11, 2011*, New York: Penguin Books, 2004; Joseph E. Persico, *Casey: The Lives and Secrets of William J. Casey: From OSS to the CIA*, New York: Penguin Books, 1991.

mix of coethnic sentiment, special operations activities, and conventional deterrence to annex Crimea and destabilize eastern Ukraine.[6] Some Baltic officials, sensitive to the presence of substantial Russian minorities in their own countries, are anxious over what might come next.[7]

Iran has skillfully employed its own special warfare capabilities as part of a long-term regional special warfare strategy, using state and nonstate proxies to advance its regional interests.[8] Iran's actions in Syria, for example, have contributed to a vexing dilemma for the United States, in which both action and inaction threaten policy disaster: the former an Iraq-style quagmire and the latter an uncontrolled regionalization of Sunni-Shi'a sectarian conflict. The Syria dilemma is symptomatic of Iran's broader efforts to establish a sphere of influence in the Middle East through mechanisms that ingrain instability in the structure of sectarian interrelations, exemplified by the patronage of such clients as Hezbollah and Quds Force activities in Iraq and other Arab states. Coupled with its quest for nuclear capability, Iran risks a cascading proliferation of nuclear weapons in a deeply divided region. In the longer term, if Iran's quest for, and Russia's exercise of, nuclear deterrence and irregular influence are seen as successful asymmetric strategies for circumventing U.S. conventional dominance, other regional or aspiring global powers might adopt similar approaches to securing their interests.

The United States should consider using special warfare campaigns to counter the aggressive employment of proxies by states competing for regional influence. Although there is no obligation for the United States to fight its adversaries symmetrically, adversaries are challenging it in ways that are difficult to credibly deter with conven-

---

[6] Robert Haddick, "The Pentagon Needs a New Way of War," *War on the Rocks*, March 18, 2014.

[7] Griff Witte, "After Russian Moves in Ukraine, Eastern Europe Shudders, NATO to Increase Presence," *Washington Post*, April 18, 2014.

[8] David Crist, *The Twilight War: The Secret History of America's Thirty-Year Conflict with Iran*, New York: Penguin, 2013; Jim Thomas and Chris Dougherty, *Beyond the Ramparts: The Future of U.S. Special Operations Forces*, Washington, D.C.: Center for Strategic and Budgetary Assessments, 2013.

tional campaigns or precision strikes alone.[9] If the United States were to rebalance its dependence on precision-strike, conventional, and special warfare capabilities—and how they complement one another— it might constitute a change in strategic posture analogous to the shift from Eisenhower's New Look dependence on massive nuclear retaliation for deterrence to Kennedy's Flexible Response goal of deterring aggression at multiple levels of the escalation ladder.[10]

To advance thinking about special warfare, this report (1) describes the unique characteristics of special warfare campaigns, (2) identifies the strategic advantages and risks associated with special warfare, (3) explores how special warfare campaigns could be used to address challenges identified in strategic guidance, (4) adapts operational art to the unique characteristics of special warfare, and (5) provides recommendations to military and civilian leaders and planners in designing and executing these campaigns. Our findings and recommendations are based on semistructured interviews with special warfare practitioners and researchers, observed military exercises, a review of the relevant literature and case studies, a review of country and theater campaign plans, and analysis of a data set of special warfare operations that our team constructed for this study.

Characteristics of Special Warfare

Special warfare campaigns, properly conducted, are far more than a SOF activity. They involve the comprehensive orchestration of U.S. government capabilities to advance policy objectives. Special warfare campaigns

- stabilize or destabilize the targeted regime

---

[9]   Karl P. Mueller, Jeffrey Martini, and Thomas Hamilton, *Airpower Options for Syria: Assessing Objectives and Missions for Aerial Intervention*, Santa Monica, Calif.: RAND Corporation, RR-446-CMEPP, 2013.

[10]   Forrest E. Morgan, Karl P. Mueller, Evan S. Medeiros, Kevin L. Pollpeter, and Roger Cliff, *Dangerous Thresholds: Managing Escalation in the 21st Century*, Santa Monica, Calif.: RAND Corporation, MG-614-AF, 2008.

- employ local partners as the main effort
- maintain a small U.S. footprint in the targeted country
- are typically of long duration and may require extensive preparatory work better measured in months (or years) than days
- require intensive interagency cooperation; U.S. Department of Defense (DoD) efforts may be subordinate to DoS or the Central Intelligence Agency (CIA)
- employ "political warfare" methods to mobilize, neutralize, or integrate individuals or groups from the tactical to the strategic levels.

The term *political warfare* has fallen out of fashion since the end of the Cold War, so it warrants some explanation. George Kennan defined it in 1948 as "all the means at a nation's command, short of war, to achieve its national objectives,"[11] though perhaps it should be interpreted as "short of conventional or nuclear war." In many ways, the concept of political warfare fits within Nye's concept of "smart power."[12] Activities range from influence operations and political action to economic sanctions and coercive diplomacy.[13] These definitions and examples are so broad as to approach all-encompassing, but a defining feature of these activities is their influence on the political coalitions that sustain or challenge power. Political warfare might be thought of as the art of making or breaking coalitions. Historically, U.S. SOF have found their comparative advantage in political warfare at the tactical level (retail politics), while other government agencies have found theirs at the strategic level. It is the political warfare element of special warfare campaigns that requires intensive interagency collaboration, creating situations in which the joint force may be supporting a DoS- or CIA-led effort.

[11] David F. Rudgers, "The Origins of Covert Action," *Journal of Contemporary History,* Vol. 35, No. 2, 2000.

[12] Joseph S. Nye, *The Future of Power,* New York: PublicAffairs, 2011.

[13] Joseph D. Celeski, *Political Warfare and Political Violence—War by Other Means,* unpublished manuscript, undated.

The challenge of proxy conflict presented by Iran and Russia is not the only reason to refine U.S. special warfare capabilities. Special warfare has much broader application for reasons of efficacy and efficiency. The past decade and a half of conflict have illustrated the need for better approaches to complex engagements in the "human domain." For example, special warfare campaigns will be an important option for post-2014 U.S. engagement in Afghanistan, as well as for addressing serious threats to U.S. national security interests in cases in which large-scale conflict is inappropriate, such as in Yemen or Libya. Moreover, a series of events and changes in the policy environment—such as the 2008 financial crisis, the 2011 Budget Control Act, U.S. withdrawal from Iraq, and the drawdown in Afghanistan—have constrained resources and U.S. appetite for expensive, high-visibility interventions, increasing policymaker interest in what the 2012 defense strategic guidance calls "innovative, low-cost, and small-footprint approaches to achieve [U.S.] security objectives."[14]

Special warfare campaigns offer several advantages in furthering U.S. interests by providing options to meet these challenges. Educating policymakers and key elements of U.S. national security agencies about the proper employment of special warfare campaigns is critical to the development of informed policies and strategies for today's conflicts.

Strategic Advantages

Some advantages of special warfare include the following:[15]

---

[14] U.S. Department of Defense, *Sustaining U.S. Global Leadership: Priorities for 21st Century Defense*, Washington, D.C., January 2012, p. 3.

[15] For a broader discussion of SOF in strategic context, see Colin S. Gray, *Explorations in Strategy*, Westport, Conn.: Praeger, 1998; Lucien S. Vandenbroucke, *Perilous Options: Special Operations as an Instrument of U.S. Foreign Policy*, New York: Oxford University Press, 1993; James D. Kiras, *Special Operations and Strategy: From World War II to the War on Terrorism*, New York: Routledge, 2006; and Joseph D. Celeski, Timothy S. Slemp, and John D. Jogerst, *An Introduction to Special Operations Power: Origins, Concepts and Application*, unpublished manuscript, 2013.

- *Improved understanding and shaping of the environment.* Special warfare, executed through intelligence or selected military activities, can improve contextual understanding of potential partners and "ground truth" before the United States commits to a course of action.
- *Cost-imposing strategies.* Special warfare's small-footprint approach allows the United States to pursue cost-imposing strategies that force opponents to spend disproportionate resources to defend against friendly capabilities.
- *Managed escalation and credibility risk.* Given a decision to intervene, policymakers could use special warfare to avoid making commitments beyond U.S. interests. However, it will be important to carefully assess the escalation criteria and options of adversaries and their external partners.
- *Sustainable solutions.* Sustainability has two components—fiscal and political. Special warfare's small-footprint approach can be more fiscally and politically sustainable than alternatives when underlying sources of conflict cannot be resolved in the short term, preserving core U.S. interests at costs that the nation is willing to bear. From a host-nation or coalition political perspective, commanders can also use special warfare's partner-centric approach to design campaigns around a partner's core interests, rather than hoping to transform them in ways that have frequently proven to be ephemeral.

Limits and Risks

As noted earlier, special warfare campaigns are characterized by operations in which the local partner provides the main effort. This dependency on partners carries a set of risks and limitations, as do other characteristics of special warfare. The following are some examples:

- *Divergent partner objectives.* A partner may have core objectives that conflict with those of the United States, or it may simply prioritize them differently.

- *Ineffective partner capability.* The opponent's level of capability and operational tempo relative to the partner's may render special warfare solutions ineffective within the required time horizon.
- *Unacceptable partner behavior.* Some partners may behave in ways that transgress U.S. normative standards (e.g., respect for human rights) and undermine their own sources of legitimacy.
- *Policy fratricide.* If special warfare campaigns are not carefully integrated into a holistic U.S. policy toward the targeted country, U.S. efforts can either come into direct conflict or fall out of balance.
- *Disclosure.* The global proliferation of information technology erodes the ability to keep covert activities covert.[16]

Although the United States might avoid some of these risks by acting unilaterally, it would lose the strategic advantages identified here.

Operational Art in Special Warfare

According to joint doctrine, operational art is "the cognitive approach by commanders and staffs—supported by their skill, knowledge, experience, creativity, and judgment—to develop strategies, campaigns and operations to organize and employ military forces by integrating ends, ways and means."[17] It is not sufficient for operational commanders and planners in a combatant or service component command to be proficient in only one form of operational art (e.g., major combat operations, counterinsurgency, unconventional warfare). The operational commander and planners must have expertise in all forms of operational art if they are to design successful campaigns across the full

---

[16] Although the proliferation of information technology has made keeping operations clandestine or covert more challenging, in other ways, it enables new opportunities to exercise influence activities, bringing about a more nuanced appreciation of the operating environment.

[17] U.S. Joint Chiefs of Staff, *Joint Operations*, Joint Publication 3-0, Washington, D.C., August 11, 2011b, p. GL-14.

range of military operations in modern conflicts. Failing to understand the nature of a conflict and planning for one type of campaign when quite a different type is called for will lead to problems, as the U.S. military discovered after it seized Baghdad in 2003.[18]

The principles of operational art provide the "connective tissue" between tactical actions and strategic objectives by supporting the design of successful campaigns. In the language of joint doctrine, we propose that *special warfare's unique contribution to operational art consists of the mobilization of partners' strategic and operational centers of gravity, and the neutralization or integration of the enemy's, in the human domain.* Joint doctrine's (somewhat unilluminating) definition of a center of gravity is "the source of power that provides a belligerent with the moral or physical strength, freedom of action, or will to act." At the strategic level, a center of gravity is best conceptualized as the source of will to implement the policy being pursued through the conflict. At the operational level, a center of gravity should be understood as the entity through which the strategic center of gravity is principally exercising its will (e.g., the possessor of critical capabilities).

The virtues of this conception of special warfare operational art are twofold. First, keeping special warfare within the joint operational art construct enables greater SOF–conventional force collaboration. Second, it should help special warfare practitioners focus beyond the achievement of tactical effects and think holistically about the integration of joint and interagency capabilities as called for in their doctrine and traditions. Special warfare's contribution to operational art must be understood in the context of a dynamic competition with an adversary, rather than through an exclusive focus on target lists or partner security force end-strength objectives that can easily be quantified.

---

[18] See Antulio J. Echevarria II, "American Operational Art, 1917–2008," in John Olsen and Martin van Creveld, eds., *The Evolution of Operational Art*, New York: Oxford University Press, 2011, pp. 137–165.

Recommendations

Providing policymakers with a credible special warfare campaign capability requires a variety of efforts by the institutional military, operating forces, geographic combatant commands, and policymakers. The following recommendations should facilitate the development of a common intellectual framework for thinking about special warfare, and making related strategic, operational, and investment decisions. We begin by identifying each problem and its root cause.

Educating Planners: Strengthen Special Warfare Strategic and Operational Planning Capabilities

DoD special warfare planning capabilities are immature. A high-priority country plan reviewed for this study revealed important misunderstandings of the elements of campaign design, such as distinctions between strategic and operational centers of gravity and between centers of gravity and critical requirements. These distinctions are more than academic when they facilitate a propensity to start with a preferred target list and plan backward from there. A target list is not a strategy, and treating it as such risks encouraging the default employment of capabilities organic to the planner's organization, rather than critical thought regarding how a joint or interagency approach might be employed to secure U.S. interests, or how host-nation nonmilitary capabilities might be leveraged.

Furthermore, special warfare campaign planners are not actively managed, and conventional planners receive limited exposure to special warfare planning challenges. Several SOF graduates of the Army's premier campaign planning school, the School of Advanced Military Studies at Fort Leavenworth, noted that enrollment was not encouraged and that prolonged separation from special forces groups generated significant career risk. A theater special operations command (TSOC) tour while still a major may be an important developmental experience for SOF campaign planners following graduation from the school (or after an intervening group tour). The John F. Kennedy Special Warfare Center and School's Unconventional Warfare Operational Design Course and the Special Operations, Operational Art Module, associated with the School of Advanced Military Studies are steps in the right direction but would likely benefit from greater joint, TSOC, and interagency engagement and influence. Currently, there appears to be no structured path for building special warfare strategists, for instance, through the U.S. Army War College's Basic Strategic Arts Program coupled with additional special warfare–specific education.

Strengthening U.S. special warfare strategic and operational planning capabilities will require improvements in the education, professional development, and career management of the special warfare planners on whose expertise these campaigns will depend. DoD should develop a viable career track for campaign planners and strategists from within the SOF community, building on best practices from the conventional military planning community but also building special warfare–unique expertise. The health of this career track will require senior leader attention and monitoring within the SOF community (e.g., of promotion rates, utilization tour trends, and active debates in the professional literature). Creating a professional association for special warfare campaign planners and strategists would be a useful aid to foster both professional standards and innovation.

Educating Joint Organizations: Develop a Special Warfare Planning Culture

In recent special warfare planning efforts, there has been insufficient collaboration between SOF and conventional force planners. SOF rarely have all the organic capabilities required for a campaign and will frequently fall under a joint task force, making the development of a joint special warfare planning culture critical. Special warfare campaigns are inherently joint, yet SOF and conventional forces lack a common understanding of special warfare and operational art.

Creating a joint special warfare planning culture will require the education of planners and commanders in the combatant commands, the Office of the Secretary of Defense, the Joint Staff, and the military services about the strengths, limits, and requirements of special warfare. Such a planning culture should include enhanced norms governing how operational objectives relate to policy objectives, assessments that are clearly linked to the commander's theory of the campaign, an enhanced focus on campaign continuity and transition planning, and recognition that precrisis efforts to prevent conflict or set conditions for conflict resolution ("shaping" activities, in the joint lexicon) should be treated seriously as decisive campaigns. These shaping campaigns will have characteristics quite different from conventional campaigns. Gaps and tensions among joint, Army, and SOF doctrine will need to be resolved.

One of the great strengths of SOF is the deference paid to the greater situational awareness of commanders on the ground. However, guidance coming from operational headquarters is sometimes so broad as to enable subordinate commanders to focus their tactical operations wherever they see fit, resulting in a lack of unity of effort and significant discontinuity across changes in command. If each unit is allowed to pursue its own priorities, even dramatic local successes are unlikely to amount to more than a series of disconnected tactical events. If special warfare campaigns are to be successful, they need strategic and operational focus.

Educating U.S. Government Stakeholders: Institutionalize Unified Action

A standard complaint among operational-level planners (e.g., combatant command and TSOC planners) is that they do not receive clear policy guidance. Seeking to design campaigns to achieve policy objectives without a clear understanding of what those policy objectives are can be a frustrating and potentially fruitless exercise.[19]

Policymakers understandably seek to understand the full import of their options, and to preserve their options for as long as possible, before committing themselves to a particular course of action. Special warfare commanders and planners should seek to help policymakers explore the implications of setting particular strategic objectives through the development of multiple options, including "off-ramps" (i.e., branches and sequels) that allow policymakers room to maneuver as conditions (and preferences) change. Policymakers, in turn, should recognize that the best way to preserve decision space is not always to

---

[19] Rosa Brooks, "Obama vs. the Generals," *Politico*, November 2013.

defer decisions but, rather, to recognize when critical investments need to be made early on to preserve options for later.

Creating the conditions for the "unified action" of U.S. government stakeholders is critical to the conduct of special warfare, since many of the most important capabilities reside outside the military. Even more so than in the joint community, focused effort will be required to educate key stakeholders on the strengths, limits, and requirements of special warfare. Key stakeholders may include country team members, regional and country desk officers, and directors at DoS, the CIA, the U.S. Agency for International Development, the National Security Council, and other organizations that may reside outside the U.S. government. During the development of specific campaigns, active engagement with policymakers will be crucial to developing the proper alignment of ends, ways, and means. Engagements with partner agencies and policymakers in times of crisis are unlikely to be successful unless foundational relationships have already been established.

Particular focus should be placed on creating an interagency mechanism for special warfare policy coordination, establishing a commonly acceptable assessment framework, and determining what constitutes adequate policy guidance.

Providing Special Warfare Options: Develop Capabilities to Prevail Among the People

Unity of effort behind the right strategy and plan is necessary but insufficient for the successful execution of a special warfare campaign. Theater commanders need access to the requisite capabilities for the campaign's execution. The past decade and a half of war in Afghanistan and Iraq has degraded the depth of regional and country expertise in the SOF community and, to a lesser extent, the functional expertise required for special warfare. There are several initiatives that the SOF community can undertake to enhance the credibility of special warfare options for addressing strategic dilemmas. New investments in people, organizations, and intellectual capital will need to be made.

Preparing for the next special warfare campaign will require some refocusing for the SOF generation that matured during the

Iraq, Afghanistan, and global counterterrorism campaigns of the past decade and a half. Continued war-gaming and training exercises over a broader range of scenarios than those encountered in recent theaters will help commanders identify where organizational and doctrinal change is required.

To provide a mature capability appropriate for the execution of a special warfare campaign, the SOF community should consider establishing a general officer–level operational headquarters element, similar to the division or corps level of conventional units. During operations in Afghanistan, in particular, the breadth of responsibilities within the special operations community steadily drove up the requirement for a higher-echelon command-and-control organization. These responsibilities included security force assistance, direct action, the initiation and management of innovative programs (e.g., village stability operations), and the coordination of diverse SOF (e.g., special forces, civil affairs, military information support), multinational, and host-nation efforts. The SOF command-and-control architecture evolved in an ad hoc way over the course of more than a decade, and it inhibited commanders' ability to adequately participate in theater-level planning.

The core contribution of special warfare to operational art is the mobilization, neutralization, or integration of operational and strategic centers of gravity in the human domain ("among the people," in General Sir Rupert Smith's words).[20] Influence capabilities at the operational level will be critical for the conduct of special warfare campaigns. Influence activities at the operational level are insufficiently mature. Research and concept development beyond current military information support activities is required and should include the development of political warfare concepts. Applying influence concepts, and special warfare more generally, in a specific campaign will require more than the regional expertise developed in some parts of the SOF community, leading us to recommend enhanced country-level expertise for selected countries of strategic significance. This additional expertise

---

[20] Rupert Smith, *The Utility of Force: The Art of War in the Modern World*, New York: Alfred A. Knopf, 2005.

should be organizationally buttressed by the creation of "green" and "white" intelligence capabilities for nonlethal targeting and analysis.

Conclusion

Special warfare will sometimes be the most effective way for the United States to achieve its strategic goals. Given recent trends in Europe and the Middle East, this will likely be the case with increasing frequency. When the United States pursues its interests through special warfare, it will require a different conceptual model for the design and conduct of campaigns than what the joint force is accustomed to. This is because special warfare works principally through local actors, employs political warfare methods, and requires the integration of a much broader suite of U.S. government agency capabilities than is typically envisioned in conventional campaigns. As a result, the U.S. national security community needs to begin thinking seriously about special warfare capabilities, authorities, options, and risks in strategic and operational planning.

Acknowledgments

We thank LTG Charles T. Cleveland, then commanding general of U.S. Army Special Operations Command (USASOC), for sponsoring this project and for his guidance. COL Timothy Fitzgerald and Paul Tompkins at USASOC and MAJ Andrew Basquez at U.S. Army Special Forces Command provided invaluable guidance and subject-matter expertise. Jim Lane and Matt Erlacher at USASOC provided excellent support and assistance to this research.

This report greatly benefited from the thoughtful insights of MG Christopher K. Haas, LTC (ret.) Mark Grdovic, COL (ret.) Joe Celeski, COL Pat Mahaney, LTC Thomas Matelski, LTC Derek Jones, LTC Michael Kenny, Sean Ryan, and many more than can be listed here. Thanks to MAJ Ryan Agee and CWO Maurice Duclos for allowing us to build on their unconventional warfare data set. This report also greatly benefited from the insights of our RAND colleagues Arturo Muñoz, Mark Sparkman, James Quinlivan, Seth Jones, and Charles Ries.

We are grateful to the director of RAND Arroyo Center's Strategy and Resources Program, Terrence Kelly, for his valuable feedback and encouragement, as well as to Jon Welch for his work developing our special warfare data set, Matt Boyer for facilitating many of our engagements with the special operations community, and Cassandra Tate for her excellent administrative support.

Finally, thanks to the reviewers of this report: COL (ret.) Dave Maxwell, Thomas McNaugher, and Douglas Ollivant. Their suggestions and insights greatly improved the quality of this work.

Abbreviations

APEX	Adaptive Planning and Execution system
CIA	Central Intelligence Agency
DoD	U.S. Department of Defense
DoS	U.S. Department of State
DRA	Democratic Republic of Afghanistan
ESAF	El Salvador Armed Forces
FID	foreign internal defense
FM	field manual
FMLN	Farabundo Martí National Liberation Front
GCC	geographic combatant command
ISI	Pakistani Inter-Services Intelligence directorate
ISR	intelligence, surveillance, and reconnaissance
JCET	Joint Combined Exchange Training
JIIM	joint, interagency, intergovernmental, and multinational
JP	joint publication
JSPS	Joint Strategic Planning System

MOE	measure of effectiveness
MOP	measure of performance
PDPA	People's Democratic Party of Afghanistan
PE	preparation of the environment
POM	program objective memorandum
SFA	security force assistance
SOF	special operations forces
TSOC	theater special operations command
UN	United Nations
USAID	U.S. Agency for International Development
USASOC	U.S. Army Special Operations Command
USSOCOM	U.S. Special Operations Command
VEO	violent extremist organization

CHAPTER ONE

Introduction

Purpose and Motivation

In the face of adversaries exploiting regional social cleavages through the use of special operations forces (SOF) and intelligence services, coupled with a dwindling appetite for intervention, the United States needs to employ a more sophisticated form of special warfare to secure its interests.[1] Special warfare campaigns stabilize a friendly state or destabilize a hostile regime by operating "through and with" local state or nonstate partners, rather than through unilateral U.S. action. SOF

---

[1] Special warfare consists of "activities that involve a combination of lethal and nonlethal actions taken by a specially trained and educated force that has a deep understanding of cultures and foreign language, proficiency in small-unit tactics, and the ability to build and fight alongside indigenous combat formations in a permissive, uncertain, or hostile environment." It includes "special operations forces conducting combinations of unconventional warfare, foreign internal defense, and/or counterinsurgency through and with indigenous forces or personnel" (Headquarters, U.S. Department of the Army, *Special Operations*, Army Doctrine Publication 3-05, Washington, D.C., August 2012c, p. 9).

The definition of *unconventional warfare* has been contentious and has shifted over time (D. Jones, *Ending the Debate: Unconventional Warfare, Foreign Internal Defense, and Why Words Matter*, thesis, Ft. Leavenworth, Kan.: U.S. Army Command and General Staff College, 2006). DoD Directive 3000.07 defines unconventional warfare as a

> broad spectrum of military and paramilitary operations, normally of long duration, predominantly conducted through, with, or by indigenous or surrogate forces who are organized, trained, equipped, supported, and directed in varying degrees by an external source. It includes, but is not limited to, guerrilla warfare, subversion, sabotage, intelligence activities, and unconventional assisted recovery. (U.S. Department of Defense Directive 3000.07, *Irregular Warfare (IW)*, December 1, 2008)

In this study, we use the current joint definition of *unconventional warfare*.

are the primary U.S. military forces employed, but successful campaigns depend on a broad suite of joint and U.S. government capabilities. Special warfare has particular relevance to the current global security environment as policymakers seek options short of large-scale intervention to manage (or assist in managing) challenges both acute (e.g., Syrian civil war, Ukraine crisis) and chronic (e.g., insurgency in the Philippines).

Special warfare fills the missing middle for exerting influence between precision-strike options provided by armed unmanned aerial systems, SOF raids, aircraft and missiles, and the costly commitment of conventional forces. The potential for escalation associated with precision-strike capabilities may render them too risky to employ in some circumstances.[2] In cases in which the targeted regime's core interests are involved, precision-strike options may be insufficient to compel desired changes in behavior.[3]

To advance thinking about special warfare, this report (1) describes the unique characteristics of special warfare, (2) identifies the strategic advantages and risks associated with special warfare, (3) explores how special warfare campaigns could be used to address challenges identi-

---

According to Joint Publication (JP) 3-05, *Special Operations,* unconventional warfare consists of

> activities conducted to enable a resistance movement or insurgency to coerce, disrupt, or overthrow a government or occupying power by operating through or with an underground, auxiliary, and guerrilla force in a denied area. (U.S. Joint Chiefs of Staff, *Special Operations,* Joint Publication 3-05, Washington, D.C., July 16, 2014, p. xi)

JP 3-22, *Foreign Internal Defense,* states,

> Foreign internal defense (FID) is the participation by civilian and military agencies of a government in any of the action programs taken by another government or other designated organization, to free and protect its society from subversion, lawlessness, insurgency, terrorism, and other threats to their security. . . . The focus of US FID efforts is to support the [host nation's] internal defense and development. . . . It focuses on building viable institutions that respond to the needs of society. (U.S. Joint Chiefs of Staff, *Foreign Internal Defense,* Joint Publication 3-22, Washington, D.C., July 12, 2010, p. ix)

[2]   David Gompert and Terrence Kelly, "Escalation Cause: How the Pentagon's New Strategy Could Trigger War with China," *Foreign Policy,* August 2, 2013.

[3]   Ivo Daalder and Michael O'Hanlon, *Winning Ugly: NATO's War to Save Kosovo,* Washington, D.C.: Brookings Institution Press, 2000.

fied in strategic guidance, and (4) adapts operational art to the unique characteristics of special warfare, and (5) provides recommendations to military and civilian leaders and planners in designing and executing these campaigns.

There is already an extensive set of doctrine on the design of joint campaigns. Rather than reproduce all the processes captured there, we focus on the specific adaptations required to understand and employ special warfare at the operational level.

Special warfare is a U.S. Army SOF doctrinal term meaning the "execution of activities that involve a combination of lethal and non-lethal actions taken by a specially trained and educated force that has a deep understanding of cultures and foreign language[s], proficiency in small-unit tactics, and the ability to build and fight alongside indigenous combat formations in a permissive, uncertain, or hostile environment," and "represents special operations forces conducting combinations of unconventional warfare, foreign internal defense, and/or counterinsurgency through and with indigenous forces or personnel."

As we discuss later at greater length, special warfare campaigns

- stabilize or destabilize the targeted regime
- employ local partners as the main effort
- maintain a small U.S. footprint in the targeted country
- are typically of long duration and may require extensive preparatory work better measured in months (or years) than in days
- require intensive interagency cooperation; for example, the U.S. Department of Defense (DoD) efforts may be subordinate to the U.S. Department of State (DoS) or the Central Intelligence Agency (CIA)
- employ "political warfare" methods to mobilize, neutralize, or integrate individuals or groups from the tactical to the strategic level.

Special warfare *campaigns* are those in which the principal activities are special warfare activities. Although their goal at the tactical or operational level is either to stabilize or destabilize, they may be conducted in support of some other strategic objective (e.g., tying up a competitor's resources, gaining access for other intelligence assets). Special warfare campaigns can be conducted in peacetime (phases 0 and 1 in the traditional campaign phase paradigm) to avoid the need for conventional military intervention. When large-scale joint operations are occurring (phases 2 and 3 and, in some cases, phase 4 of the campaign phase paradigm), special warfare activities will still be important but are unlikely to be the main effort.

Despite policymaker antipathy toward the costs and risks of intervention, instability observed and forecast in the global environment will continue to create situations in which policymakers may feel forced to act to protect U.S. interests.[4] As mentioned earlier, the escalation risk associated with deep-strike capabilities may render them too risky to employ coercively.[5] When the targeted regime's core interests are involved, they may be insufficient to unilaterally compel desired changes in behavior.[6]

Special warfare is not new. The United States has a long (and somewhat checkered) history of special warfare operations. Classic cases from the 1980s include U.S. support to the government of El Salvador against the Farabundo Martí National Liberation Front (FMLN) Marxist insurgents and to the Mujahedeen in Afghanistan against the Soviets. In the former case, the U.S. military was restricted to providing no more than 55 advisers, who did not participate in combat operations. In the latter case, operations were conducted almost entirely from and through a third country, Pakistan.[7] Today, operations in Colombia and the Philippines constitute classic cases of special warfare. However, more than a decade of focus on counterterrorism, Iraq, and Afghanistan has atrophied U.S. special warfare campaign design

---

[4] National Intelligence Council, *Global Trends 2030: Alternative Worlds*, Washington, D.C., 2012.

[5] Gompert and Kelly, 2013.

[6] Daalder and O'Hanlon, 2000.

[7] Steve Coll, *Ghost Wars: The Secret History of the CIA, Afghanistan, and bin Laden, from the Soviet Invasion to September 11, 2011*, New York: Penguin Books, 2004; Joseph E. Persico, *Casey: The Lives and Secrets of William J. Casey: From OSS to the CIA*, New York: Penguin Books, 1991.

skills in the military and appreciation for special warfare's employment as a strategic tool in the policy community. This report provides an intellectual framework for integrating the planning efforts of special operations and conventional forces, the combatant commands, DoS, the intelligence community, and policymakers.

The United States is not the only country with special warfare capabilities. Iran has skillfully employed these capabilities as part of a regional special warfare strategy, using state and nonstate proxies to advance its regional interests.[8] Iran's actions in Syria, for example, have contributed to a vexing dilemma for the United States, in which both action and inaction threaten policy disaster: the former an Iraq-style quagmire and the latter an uncontrolled regionalization of Sunni-Shi'a sectarian conflict. The Syria dilemma is symptomatic of Iran's broader efforts to establish a sphere of influence in the Middle East through mechanisms that ingrain instability into the structure of sectarian interrelations, exemplified by the patronage of such clients such as Hezbollah and Quds Force activities in Iraq and other Arab states. Coupled with its quest for nuclear capability, Iran risks a cascading pro-liferation of nuclear weapons in a deeply divided region. In the longer term, if Iran's quest for nuclear deterrence and irregular influence is seen as a successful asymmetric strategy for circumventing U.S. con-ventional dominance, other regional or aspiring global powers might adopt similar approaches to securing their interests. The United States might consider using special warfare campaigns to counter the aggres-sive employment of proxies by states competing for regional influence.

The challenge of proxy conflict presented by Iran and Russia is not the only reason to refine U.S. special warfare capabilities. Special warfare has much broader application for reasons of efficacy and effi-ciency (see Figure 1.1). The past decade and a half of conflict have illus-trated the need for better approaches to complex engagements in the "human domain." For example, special warfare campaigns will be an

---

[8] David Crist, *The Twilight War: The Secret History of America's Thirty-Year Conflict with Iran*, New York: Penguin, 2013; Jim Thomas and Chris Dougherty, *Beyond the Ramparts: The Future of U.S. Special Operations Forces*, Washington, D.C.: Center for Strategic and Budget-ary Assessments, 2013.

Figure 1.1
SOF Core Operations and Capabilities

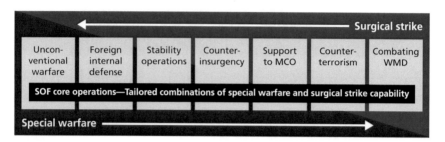

SOURCE: U.S. Army Special Operations Command, *ARSOF 2022: The Future Operation Environment*, Washington, D.C.: Headquarters, U.S. Department of the Army, undated, p. 11.

NOTES: MCO = major combat operation. WMD = weapons of mass destruction.

RAND *RR779-1.1*

important option for U.S. engagement in Afghanistan, as well as for addressing serious threats to U.S. national security interests in cases in which large-scale conflict is inappropriate, such as in Yemen or Libya.

Moreover, major events and changes in the policy environment—such as the 2008 financial crisis, the 2011 Budget Control Act, U.S. withdrawal from Iraq, and the drawdown in Afghanistan—have constrained resources and U.S. appetite for expensive, high-visibility interventions, increasing policymaker interest in what the 2012 defense strategic guidance calls "innovative, low-cost, and small-footprint approaches to achieve [U.S.] security objectives."[9]

Special warfare as a policy tool for addressing both state and nonstate threats fills an important and complementary role between diplomacy and conventional interventions. Special warfare capabilities should prove an important contribution to the joint community's ability to meet strategic guidance, address the challenges of the current and foreseeable operating environment, and maintain the military's relevance to policymaker needs.

---

[9]   U.S. Department of Defense, *Sustaining U.S. Global Leadership: Priorities for 21st Century Defense*, Washington, D.C., January 2012, p. 3.

Method and Organization of This Report

To develop a baseline understanding of the problems involved with special warfare operational art, the study team

- conducted semistructured interviews with special warfare practitioners and researchers from a variety of organizational backgrounds (e.g., special forces, conventional forces, CIA, DoS)
- attended U.S. Army Special Operations Command exercises
- conducted a review of the relevant literature, including doctrine, case studies, lessons learned, country plans, and academic literature
- constructed a data set of special warfare operations (for additional detail, see Appendix D in the companion volume to this report).

We used this review as a basis for the analysis of special warfare's unique characteristics, how those features influence the conduct of operational art, and what obstacles exist to the exercise of special warfare campaigns at the operational level.

We then applied our construct to two cases (one FID, one unconventional warfare) to assess whether they furthered understanding of operational art in the special warfare context. In these case studies, we addressed three key questions:

1. Does the application of new concepts illuminate key factors in the campaign's success or failure otherwise lost in the classic model of campaigning and operational art?
2. Are these concepts clear and parsimonious enough to be readily incorporated into current doctrine, education, and training without causing confusion?
3. Are these concepts individually necessary and collectively sufficient to explain outcomes?

The remainder of this report is organized as follows. Chapter Two describes the nuts and bolts of special warfare (the "what") and frames its significance at the policy level (the "so what?").[10] In Chapter Three, we develop the conceptual foundations of operational art in special warfare and describe its integration with joint operational art. In Chapter Four, we provide a guide to navigating some of the key challenges in organizing for special warfare in the joint, interagency, intergovernmental, and multinational (JIIM) contexts (the "how").[11] In Chapter Five, we use two historical case studies (the conflicts in Afghanistan and El Salvador in the 1980s) and a notional future scenario to ground intuitions about how the special warfare style of operational art is distinct from conventional operational art. Chapter Six, concludes the report and offers recommendations derived from our analyses.

The second volume of this report, *Toward Operational Art in Special Warfare: Appendixes* (available online at www.rand.org/t/RR779), offers additional context to supplement the discussions presented here. Appendix A in that volume provides a brief overview of the evolution of operational art. Appendix B summarizes the literature on developing consensus among groups or individuals with disparate goals and approaches and explains how this could be used in special warfare planning. Appendix C reviews the resources and authorities for special warfare. Appendix D provides additional details on our data set of special warfare campaigns conducted by the United States since World War II. Appendix E presents notional special warfare campaigns that might be used to train special warfare campaign planners and assist DoD in identifying capability requirements for special warfare campaigns. Appendix F explores in greater depth the SOF activity "preparation of the environment." Finally, Appendix G offers a detailed discussion of the recommendations presented in Chapter Six of this report.

---

[10] We provide a broader exploration of the relevance of special warfare to the current global security environment and strategic guidance through a series of notional campaign types in Appendix E in the companion volume.

[11] Rather than reproducing current joint planning doctrine, we offer this section as a practical resource to dealing with the real-world challenges of planning in the JIIM environment, where guidance can be unclear (or nonexistent) and "unified action" is frequently aspirational at best.

CHAPTER TWO

Understanding Special Warfare

This chapter provides background information on special warfare. Specifically, it reviews the doctrinal definitions of special warfare and associated operations, briefly explores the universe of U.S. cases, and identifies the unique characteristics of special warfare that are relevant to campaign planning. Building on this foundational knowledge, we explore special warfare's contribution to operational art in Chapter Three.

Defining Special Warfare and Operational Art

As mentioned in Chapter One, special warfare is the "execution of activities that involve a combination of lethal and nonlethal actions taken by a specially trained and educated force that has a deep understanding of cultures and foreign language, proficiency in small-unit tactics, and the ability to build and fight alongside indigenous combat formations in a permissive, uncertain, or hostile environment."[1]

Doctrinal characterizations of special warfare can be decomposed into missions (ends), methods (ways), forces employed (means), and the operating environment.

- Special warfare missions include unconventional warfare, FID, counterinsurgency, stability operations, special reconnaissance, and security force assistance (SFA). Of these, FID, counterinsur-

---

[1] Headquarters, U.S. Department of the Army, 2012c, p. 9.

gency, stability operations, and unconventional warfare are considered Army SOF "core operations."

- *Method* is characterized as "a combination of lethal and nonlethal actions" and conducted primarily "through and with indigenous forces and personnel."[2]
- Forces that conduct special warfare are characterized ambiguously in the professional literature. Sometimes, *special warfare* is characterized as "an umbrella term that represents special operations forces conducting combinations [of the above missions]," while the missions themselves are can be defined as "comprehensive civilian and military efforts" (e.g., counterinsurgency).[3]
- The operating environment is usually characterized in DoD and service-level doctrine as "permissive, uncertain, or hostile"—that is, not restricted to times of overt conflict.

Special warfare is also contrasted with "surgical-strike" capabilities that are unilateral in nature and optimized for such missions as counterterrorism and hostage rescue. The explicit doctrinal definition of special warfare focuses only on the ways and means; it does not mention ends—the mission (e.g., unconventional warfare, counterterrorism).[4]

As defined in doctrine, counterinsurgency and stability operations could be considered forms of FID conducted primarily by U.S., rather than partner, forces. To more clearly highlight the unique contributions of special warfare operational art, we concentrated on unconventional warfare and FID campaigns in which the local partner force was the main effort.

Unconventional warfare consists of "activities conducted to enable a resistance movement or insurgency to coerce, disrupt, or overthrow a government or occupying power by operating through or with

---

[2]   Headquarters, U.S. Department of the Army, 2012c, p. 9.

[3]   Headquarters, U.S. Department of the Army, 2012c, p. 9.

[4]   See Headquarters, U.S. Department of the Army, 2012c; and Headquarters, U.S. Department of the Army, *Special Operations*, Army Doctrine Reference Publication 3-05, Washington, D.C., August 2012d.

an underground, auxiliary, and guerrilla force in a denied area."[5] The unconventional warfare campaign in Afghanistan in the 1980s is an example of a campaign with objectives that gradually evolved, from disrupting the Soviets to coercing them to withdraw their forces to ultimately overthrowing the Najibullah regime. Among other objectives, the U.S. unconventional warfare campaign in Tibet in the 1950s and 1960s was intended to disrupt Chinese control and force the Chinese to commit additional forces that might otherwise be free for other missions. The definition of *unconventional warfare* has been contentious, and it has shifted over time.[6] Despite considerable debate in the professional literature, confusion remains over the definition of unconventional warfare.[7] In this study, we use the current joint definition. Its central feature is the use of a local partner force to challenge an incumbent regime, though "force" should be understood loosely here to include underground, auxiliary, *or* guerrilla forces. The challenge to the incumbent regime may to overthrow it, or it may be restrained to more limited objectives, such as coercing a change in policy over the treatment of ethnic minorities or disrupting illicit smuggling networks.

FID is sometimes mistakenly seen as limited to the sporadic exercises and security cooperation activities conducted in noncrisis situations, but, in fact, it ranges from those military-focused peacetime engagements to far more comprehensive efforts. As mentioned in Chapter One, FID is the

> participation by civilian and military agencies of a government in any of the action programs taken by another government or other designated organization, to free and protect its society from subversion, lawlessness, insurgency, terrorism, and other threats to their security. . . . The focus of US FID efforts is to support the

---

[5]   U.S. Joint Chiefs of Staff, 2014, p. xi.

[6]   D. Jones, 2006. For instance, the definition in DoD Directive 3000.07 (2008), provided in Chapter One, is much broader than the current doctrinal definition.

[7]   It is not unusual to hear practitioners discuss "high-end" or "black" unconventional warfare operations, though others feel these distinctions add to the conceptual confusion (Mark Grdovic, "Developing a Common Understanding of Unconventional Warfare," *Joint Force Quarterly*, No. 57, 2nd Quarter 2010; research team's observations, January 23, 2013).

[host-nation's] internal defense and development. . . . It focuses on building viable institutions that respond to the needs of society.[8]

FID and unconventional warfare are mirror images of one another. While FID typically seeks to bolster the legitimacy of the host nation, unconventional warfare typically seeks to degrade it.

Operational art "is the pursuit of strategic objectives, in whole or in part, through the arrangement of tactical actions in time, space, and purpose."[9] It involves the "creative thinking by commanders and staffs to design strategies, campaigns, and major operations and organize and employ military forces."[10] Luttwak describes it as the "concerted use of tactical means to achieve operational-level results that are much more than the sum of the (tactical) parts."[11]

All of these definitions imply that clearly defined tasks will be required to execute a campaign if the tactical means are to support campaign objectives.[12] The political nature of objectives in special warfare often makes the assignment of clear tasks challenging for commanders and planners. It also complicates the process of conducting assessments, making them more dependent on the judgment of commanders on the ground. The need for greater situational awareness among commanders on the ground takes on additional significance in special warfare, which, to some degree, compresses the relationship between the strategic and operational levels of war.

The Army's AirLand Battle doctrine is widely regarded as a superlative refinement of conventional operational art, what Echevarria calls

[8] U.S. Joint Chiefs of Staff, 2010, p. ix.

[9] Headquarters, U.S. Department of the Army, *Unified Land Operations*, Army Doctrine Publication 3-0, Washington, D.C., May 2012b, p. 9.

[10] U.S. Joint Chiefs of Staff, *Joint Operations*, Joint Publication 3-0, Washington, D.C., August 11, 2011b, p. xii.

[11] Edward N. Luttwak, "The Operational Level of War," *International Security*, Vol. 5, No. 3, Winter 1980–1981, p. 63.

[12] A difficulty encountered by Israel Defense Forces in Lebanon in 2006, when it attempted to employ a poorly understood doctrinal concept called Systemic Operational Design (David E. Johnson, Michael Spirtas, and Ghassan Schbley, *Rediscovering the Full Range of Military Operations*, unpublished RAND Corporation research, 2009).

"war's first grammar." Developed to defeat the numerically superior Soviet forces in Cold War Europe by reconceptualizing an integrated battlefield on which the Air Force would shatter large formations and the Army would annihilate the remainder, its efficacy was proven in Operation Desert Storm.[13] As the 1986 Army operations field manual (FM 100-5), which brought greater emphasis to operational art in Air-Land Battle, observed,

> Reduced to its essentials, operational art requires the combatant commander to answer three questions:
> 1. What military condition must be produced to achieve the strategic goal [ends]?
> 2. What sequence of actions is most likely to produce that outcome [ways]?
> 3. How should military resources be applied to accomplish that sequence of actions [means]?[14]

Given the limited resources and uncertainties associated with war (and peace), commanders and planners will have to identify the level of risk they are assuming in answering these questions.

Because this study is focused on special warfare campaign planning (and, hence, operational art) rather than special warfare "activities" only, we require a definition of special warfare *campaigns*. Grdovic notes, "Operations are more clearly categorized by what they intend to achieve rather than by individual techniques or who is conducting them."[15] To accommodate both the doctrinal definition of special warfare and the logical categorization of operations, we posit that a campaign's end (the conditions to be produced) and the main effort's

---

[13] Antulio J. Echevarria II, "American Operational Art, 1917–2008," in John Olsen and Martin van Creveld, eds., *The Evolution of Operational Art*, New York: Oxford University Press, 2011.

[14] Headquarters, U.S. Department of the Army, *Operations*, Field Manual 100-5, Washington, D.C., May 1986, p. 10.

[15] Mark Grdovic, *A Leader's Handbook to Unconventional Warfare*, Publication 09-1, Ft. Bragg, N.C.: U.S. Army John F. Kennedy Special Warfare Center and School, November 2009, p. 9.

ways (e.g., guerrilla warfare) determine the campaign type. Means are not restricted to SOF; conventional forces or CIA, U.S. Agency for International Development (USAID), or other organizations' capabilities could be employed. Supporting efforts are not restricted to special warfare methods; direct action or other approaches could be employed. Strategic goals are also not restricted to special warfare missions; for example, Afghanistan has been prosecuted as a counterinsurgency campaign to achieve a counterterrorism objective.

This leads us to define *special warfare campaigns* as those in which *the principal ways of achieving campaign objectives are foreign internal defense and/or unconventional warfare operations, conducted principally "through and with" local partners* (see Figure 2.1).[16] A particular special warfare campaign might occur entirely in the "steady-state," peacetime environment where the United States wishes to improve or simply better understand a host-nation security capacity (to facilitate counternarcotics operations, for example), as part of a geographic combatant command's (GCC's) broader theater campaign plan, or for other reasons.

Although special warfare operations have played an important supporting role in conventional campaigns (e.g., unconventional warfare in northern Iraq during Operation Iraqi Freedom) and are likely to continue to do so, for the purposes of this study, we focused on contingencies in which special warfare was the main effort.

---

[16] Doctrinally, counterinsurgency is a special warfare mission. To more clearly focus on the unique contributions of special warfare operational art, we concentrate in this report on unconventional warfare and FID campaigns in which the local partner force was the main effort, as opposed to counterinsurgency, in which U.S. operations are typically the main effort. In principle, the development and employment of host-nation forces might be the main effort of a counterinsurgency campaign, but, in practice, this is not how the United States has conducted counterinsurgency. More importantly, there is value in maintaining a clear conceptual distinction between FID and counterinsurgency to help account for a central characteristic of campaigns as distinct as those in Colombia and Afghanistan over the past decade. Counterterrorism campaigns are orthogonal to this construct. In these campaigns, counterterrorism is the priority; affecting the stability of the operating environment is not. If a mission focuses on state stability, it becomes a FID or unconventional warfare operation (or campaign) in support of a broader (e.g., global) counterterrorism campaign. A counterterrorism operation can incorporate capabilities and methods associated with unconventional warfare, but that does not make it an unconventional warfare operation.

Figure 2.1
Local Partners and Special Warfare Campaigns

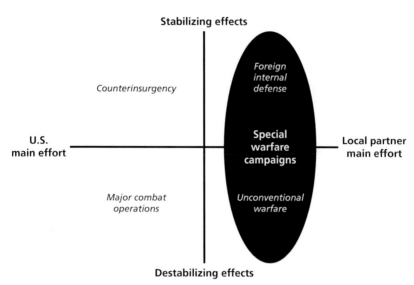

NOTE: Any type of operation can be employed as a subordinate element of any
campaign type (for example, unconventional warfare in northern Iraq during
the 2003 U.S. invasion).
RAND RR779-2.1

Selected Special Warfare Choices

Operations conducted using special warfare capabilities, whether for
unconventional warfare or FID, face key decisions at the joint task
force and, sometimes, policy levels. These decisions can be characterized as pertaining to the signature, partner, form of support, form of
aid, and the operation's role in the campaign (see Table 2.1).

An operation's signature may either be overt, low-visibility, clandestine, or covert. Overt activities are "openly acknowledged by or are
readily attributable to the United States Government." Low-visibility
operations are actually a subset of overt operations, "wherein the
political-military restrictions inherent in covert and clandestine operations are either not necessary or not feasible; actions are taken as
required to limit exposure of those involved and/or their activities."

Table 2.1
Selected Special Warfare Sponsor Choices

Decision Type	Considerations
Signature	Overt, low-visibility operations, clandestine, covert
Partner	Convention, irregular
Support	Indirect, direct, combat
Aid	Material/nonmaterial, lethal/nonlethal
Role in campaign	Main effort, supporting effort

SOURCES: Headquarters, U.S. Department of the Army, *Special Forces Unconventional Warfare*, Training Circular 18-01, January 28, 2011a; Headquarters, U.S. Department of the Army, 2012c; D. Jones, 2006.

Clandestine operations are conducted with the "intent to assure secrecy and concealment."[17] Covert operations are "planned and executed as to conceal the identity of or permit plausible denial by the sponsor." The distinction between clandestine and covert operations is a matter of some controversy because of debates over Title 50 intelligence authorities, which we address in more detail in Chapter Four. Briefly, in clandestine operations "emphasis is placed on concealment of the operation rather than on concealment of the identity of the sponsor."[18] Whether the operation is overt or covert has no bearing on whether it should be considered unconventional warfare or FID.

---

[17] This was the definition at the time of this research, in mid-2013. The definition when this report was in press was "An operation sponsored or conducted by governmental departments or agencies in such a way as to assure concealment" (U.S. Joint Chiefs of Staff, *Department of Defense Dictionary of Military and Associated Terms*, Joint Publication 1-02, Washington, D.C., November 8, 2010, as amended through October 15, 2015).

[18] It is important to note that when identifying specific reporting and funding authorities for a specific special warfare operation, the statutory definitions take precedence over doctrinal definitions. The statutory definition of *covert action* includes not only the concealment of the United States' role but also concealment of the purpose: "to influence political, economic, or military conditions abroad" (50 U.S.C. 3093e, "Covert Action" Defined). It also contains exceptions, such as "traditional military activities." Under the current doctrinal definition, therefore, an operation may be deemed covert when it is not, in fact, considered covert under current statutes. *Clandestine activity* does not have a formal statutory definition, but most relevant operations fall under "intelligence activities." See Appendix C in the companion volume for more information.

The United States may choose to partner with either conventional or irregular forces. The Civilian Irregular Defense Group program in Vietnam is an example of FID activities with an irregular partner.

U.S. support to a partner might be indirect, direct, or combat-focused. Indirect support might include the provision of security assistance or the provision of advisers through a third country (similar to, for example, Argentine support to the Contras in Nicaragua). Direct support (minus combat) might consist of advisers who are embedded in the partner force at echelons above the tactical level, military information support operations, or humanitarian assistance. Combat support could involve advisers embedded in the partner force's tactical units, engaging in direct combat operations or unilateral combat operations in support of the partner's effort (e.g., U.S. counterterrorism operations in support of a FID campaign). Unilateral operations are at odds with the philosophy underlying special warfare approaches, but they may be an appropriate part of a broader campaign.

U.S. aid to the partner might be through any of the instruments of national power, conventionally identified as diplomatic, informational, military, and economic.[19] In practice, there appear to be important inflection points in U.S. assistance: first, between materiel and nonmaterial aid, constituting a decision to move beyond rhetorical support (which, itself, can be critical) to the resourcing of support for a partner, and, second, in the decision whether to go beyond providing nonlethal aid, such as medical supplies, to providing lethal aid, such as small arms. Additional inflection points likely exist—for instance, the decision to provide weapons that may constitute a threat to friendly capabilities (e.g., Stinger missiles)—but our overview provides a useful starting point for understanding where policymakers may see important transition points in a campaign, constituting qualitative escalations in the level of U.S. commitment.

Finally, special warfare capabilities may be employed in operations that are either the main effort or the supporting effort. The unconventional warfare operation in Afghanistan in 2001 was the main effort, but in Iraq in 2003, the unconventional warfare operation in northern

---

[19] U.S. Joint Chiefs of Staff, 2010.

Iraq in which U.S. forces partnered with *peshmerga* was a supporting effort to the conventional invasion.

The local partner that the United States is supporting will have its own choices to make regarding the principal features of its campaign. Any number of frameworks might be employed to illustrate the breadth of choices available to the partner, but, for simplicity, we organize them according to elements of the Clausewitzian trinity: government, military, and population.[20] The options presented in Table 2.2 are purely illustrative and situation-dependent, not exhaustive or universal.

A FID partner might focus on defeating an insurgency through the "classic" counterinsurgency approach (also called the "ink-spot" method) elaborated in the U.S. Army and Marine Corps counterinsurgency field manual and is typically (if too simplistically) characterized as population-centric.[21] The ink-spot approach typically requires more than simply providing security to the population; it also includes delivering services and institutional reforms. More troublingly, a state with which the United States is interested in partnering might be tempted to drain Mao's proverbial sea through forced population movements, or even indiscriminate violence against populations thought to support insurgents.[22] Although

Table 2.2
Illustrative Special Warfare Partner Choices

Campaign Target	Regime/Occupying Power	Insurgency/Resistance
Population	Ink spot, "draining the sea"	Maoist protracted war, protest movement, labor strikes
Military	Attrition, attack the network	Focoist, Maoist mobile warfare
(Shadow) government	Leadership decapitation, negotiation	Subversion, sabotage

---

[20] Carl von Clausewitz, *On War*, Michael Howard and Peter Paret, trans., Princeton, N.J.: Princeton University Press, 1984.

[21] Headquarters, U.S. Department of the Army, and Headquarters, U.S. Marine Corps, *Insurgencies and Countering Insurgencies*, Field Manual 3-24/Marine Corps Warfighting Publication 3-33.5, Washington, D.C., May 2014.

[22] See Benjamin Valentino, Paul Huth, and Dylan Balch-Lindsay, "'Draining the Sea': Mass Killing and Guerrilla Warfare," *International Organization*, Vol. 58, No. 2, Spring 2004.

mass human rights violations will typically preclude U.S. support, the United States may believe it can end abuse of the population through institutional reform efforts, human rights training, and tactically embedded observers. Population-centric approaches pursued by unconventional warfare partners might include the classic form of protracted popular war developed by Mao, but nonviolent strategies might also be pursued. For example, solidarity famously contested the communist monopoly on power in Poland through the use of strikes.[23]

A FID partner seeking to focus on the military threat posed by an insurgency might choose to engage in relatively conventional assaults on known insurgent locations. Alternatively, it might seek to degrade the overall capability of the threat network by targeting key nodes (e.g., a bomb maker), an approach popularized in efforts to counter improvised explosive devices as "attacking the network." An unconventional warfare partner might seek to use military action to provide a focal point (thus, "focoism") for mobilizing the population without fostering a supportive grassroots political movement, or to simply conduct mobile (conventional) warfare without seeking to mobilize the population at all. Castro's overthrow of the Baptista dictatorship is the classic example of focoism, but most focoist efforts have failed at the operational level, and unconventional warfare partners that lack popular support in the targeted country will rarely have sufficient military power to challenge the regime conventionally.[24]

A FID partner focused on the threat "government," or leadership, might pursue a "leadership decapitation" campaign, attempting to kill off the leadership of the insurgency to break its cohesiveness.[25] Conversely, it might seek to negotiate and ultimately reconcile with the insurgent leadership. An unconventional warfare partner might seek

---

[23] Paul J. Tompkins, Jr., "Planning Considerations for Unconventional Warfare," unpublished document, Ft. Bragg, N.C.: U.S. Army Special Operations Command, 2012.

[24] Julian Schofield and Reeta Tremblay, "Why Pakistan Failed: Tribal Focoism in Kashmir," *Small Wars and Insurgencies*, Vol. 19, No. 1, March 2008.

[25] Patrick B. Johnston, "Does Decapitation Work? Assessing the Effectiveness of Leadership Targeting in Counterinsurgency Campaigns," *International Security*, Vol. 36, No. 4, Spring 2012.

to either directly subvert the government by penetrating its ministries with its own agents, as advocated by Lenin, or it might simply seek to sap the government's legitimacy through sabotage or other subversive acts.

Doctrinally, and in the broader stabilization literature, the characteristics of a regime (weak or strong), the population (segmented or homogenous), and the terrain (accessible or inaccessible) are thought to be important determinants of conflict outcomes.[26] However, the SOF community believes that certain preconflict activities can improve the prospects for a favorable conflict outcome or, more modestly, improve the quality of feasibility assessments before the United States commits to a course of action. These activities are generally referred to as *preparation of the environment* (PE).

Preparation of the environment includes "advance force operations, assessments, shaping, and intelligence activities . . . developing cultural intelligence, measuring perceptions and attitudes of the population, gaining situational awareness through area reconnaissance and media assessments, and operating covertly/clandestinely in areas where conventional forces cannot."[27] Because of widespread misunderstandings and concerns in the joint community, in the press, and among policymakers over its nature, we give extensive treatment to PE in Appendix F in the companion volume to this report.[28]

---

[26] For the doctrinal perspective, see Headquarters, U.S. Department of the Army, 2011a. The broader stabilization literature addressing this topic includes James Dobbins, Laurel E. Miller, Stephanie Pezard, Christopher Chivvis, Julie E. Taylor, Keith Crane, Calin Trenkov-Wermuth, and Tewodaj Mengistu, *Overcoming Obstacles to Peace: Local Factors in Nation-Building*, Santa Monica, Calif.: RAND Corporation, RR-167-RC, 2013; Stephen Watts, Caroline Baxter, Molly Dunigan, and Christopher Rizzi, *The Uses and Limits of Small-Scale Military Interventions*, Santa Monica, Calif.: RAND Corporation, MG-1226-RC, 2012; and Christopher Paul, Colin P. Clarke, Beth Grill, and Molly Dunigan, *Paths to Victory: Lessons from Modern Insurgencies*, Santa Monica, Calif.: RAND Corporation, RR-291/1-OSD, 2013.

[27] U.S. Joint Chiefs of Staff, 2014.

[28] Marshall Curtis Erwin, *Covert Action: Legislative Background and Possible Policy Questions*, Washington, D.C.: Congressional Research Service, April 10, 2013.

Characteristics of Special Warfare

A review of the cases and doctrine falling within our definition of special warfare campaigns reveals that such campaigns have several common features that help illuminate the challenges that operational artists must navigate. Special warfare campaigns

- stabilize or destabilize the targeted regime
- employ local partners as the main effort
- maintain a small U.S. footprint in the targeted country
- are typically long in duration and may require extensive preparatory work better measured in months (or years) than in days
- require intensive interagency cooperation; DoD may be subordinate to DoS or the CIA
- employ "political warfare" methods to mobilize, neutralize, or integrate individuals or groups from the tactical to the strategic levels.

The term *political warfare* has fallen out of fashion since the end of the Cold War, so it bears some explanation. George Kennan defined it in 1948 as "all the means at a nation's command, short of war, to achieve its national objectives,"[29] though perhaps it should be interpreted as "short of conventional or nuclear war." In many ways, the concept of political warfare fits within Nye's concept of "smart power."[30] Activities range from influence operations and political action to economic sanctions and coercive diplomacy.[31] These definitions and examples are so broad as to approach all-encompassing, but a defining feature of these activities is their influence on the political coalitions that sustain or challenge power. Political warfare might be thought of as the art of making or breaking coalitions at the international or subnational levels. Historically, U.S. SOF has found a comparative advantage in

---

[29] David F. Rudgers, "The Origins of Covert Action," *Journal of Contemporary History*, Vol. 35, No. 2, 2000.

[30] Joseph S. Nye, *The Future of Power*, New York: PublicAffairs, 2011.

[31] Joseph D. Celeski, *Political Warfare and Political Violence—War by Other Means*, unpublished manuscript, undated.

political warfare at the tactical level (retail politics), while other government agencies have found theirs at the strategic level. It is the political warfare element of special warfare campaigns that requires intensive interagency collaboration, creating situations in which the joint force may be supporting a State Department or CIA-led effort.

Special warfare campaigns may employ political warfare in the human domain to mobilize, neutralize, or integrate individuals or groups from the tactical to the strategic level. Mobilization, neutralization, and integration are explicitly political concepts in FID doctrine.[32] This might be done to strengthen relations within a critical governing (or insurgent) coalition, to degrade those relations through such mechanisms as information operations, or to alter the balance of power among groups. Political warfare can also be understood as a particular form of influence operation (a less politically sensitive term), but, unfortunately, the literature on influence operations is largely focused on influencing mass publics through informational activities and lacks mature concepts for the holistic employment of all elements of national power required to prevail in the human domain—that is, in areas in which deep understanding of the people, relationships, and balance of power "on the ground" is critical. Failing to develop concepts of employment for influence activities in the human domain is akin to developing aircraft without a strategic bombing concept, or Army formations without a concept for combined arms, to drive the identification of requirements.

Political warfare is central to the success of special warfare campaigns. Simpson observes that

> in many contemporary conflicts armed force seeks to have a direct political effect on audiences rather than setting conditions for a political solution through military effect against the enemy. . . . Whereas political considerations in war as traditionally conceived usually take place at the highest levels of military and civilian command, political considerations now drive operations even at

---

[32] Headquarters, U.S. Department of the Army, *Foreign Internal Defense*, Field Manual 3-05.2, Washington, D.C., September 2011b.

the lowest level of command: the military dimension of war is pierced by political considerations at the tactical level.[33]

Dobbins et al. identify the ability to affect geopolitical conditions and patronage networks as the critical determinants of outcomes in their review of "nation-building" cases (e.g., El Salvador, Bosnia), neither of which typically are amenable to rapid change and, in some cases, may fall beyond the mandate allotted to the task force commander, increasing the importance of a whole-of-government approach to the mission.[34] Influencing entrenched patronage networks to support the outcome desired by the United States is an important task in special warfare.[35]

The range of special warfare missions, including FID and unconventional warfare, seek to have stabilizing or destabilizing effects on a regime at the tactical or operational level. However, those campaigns may be executed with other strategic objectives. For instance, U.S. unconventional warfare operations in Tibet were conducted, at least in part, to occupy significant numbers of Chinese forces rather than to secure Tibet's independence.

The most prominent feature of special warfare is its conduct "through and with" partner forces.[36] As noted earlier, whether the United States is seeking to stabilize or destabilize a targeted state, it

---

[33] Emile Simpson, *War from the Ground Up: Twenty-First-Century Combat as Politics*, London: Hurst and Company, 2012, p. 6.

[34] Dobbins et al., 2013.

[35] Also see Eric Larson, Richard E. Darilek, Daniel Gibran, Brian Nichiporuk, Amy Richardson, Lowell H. Schwartz, and Cathryn Quantic Thurston, *Foundations of Effective Influence Operations: A Framework for Enhancing Army Capabilities*, Santa Monica, Calif.: RAND Corporation, MG-654-A, 2009, pp. xv–xvi, on the "underlying political dynamics related to achievement of U.S. coalition objectives." The researchers pose the following questions:

- What are current U.S. objectives? Are current objectives likely to be achieved, and if not, what outcomes are most likely under present or plausible conditions?
- Which actors or groups are most influential in political-military outcomes?
- What strategies (e.g., force or negotiation) are most likely to influence these groups and yield desired outcomes?
- How much authority/influence do group leaders have over their supporters/followers?

[36] Headquarters, U.S. Department of the Army, 2012c.

might choose to operate through either state or nonstate partners. The ability to leverage existent groups, or to mobilize nascent ones, is what makes special warfare an attractive option to policymakers.[37] The dependence on partner forces can keep the U.S. resource burden small, but it also presents special warfare practitioners with several risks. First, available partners must have objectives that are reconcilable with those of the United States. Second, they must have the capacity, or be capable of developing the capacity, to achieve the objectives that the United States seeks. Third, if the partner's behavior violates U.S. norms, U.S. support could be withdrawn. The employment of embedded advisers can help decisionmakers better understand partners' (and other stakeholders') objectives, assess their capacity, and monitor their behavior.

Although "footprint" is not part of the formal definition of special warfare, for campaigns that are truly "through and with" partners, we would expect the overt U.S. presence to be modest—far less than that typically required for force projection and deterrence missions.[38] During the Reagan administration, the number of military advisers assigned to El Salvador for one-year tours was congressionally limited to 55. Congress limits the number of military personnel in Colombia to 800. Following the 2002 operations in the Philippines, the SOF task force there was reduced from 1,500 to 600 personnel but has contin-

---

[37] Special warfare operational commanders and staff should be wary of attempting to manufacture resistance movements where they are not emerging organically (e.g., the Contras in Nicaragua). A similar argument could be made for investing resources in security partners without a commitment to needed reforms.

[38] Watts et al. (2012, p. 11) define the size of "minimalist stabilization" as "less than one-tenth of the doctrinally accepted force-to-population ratio of 20 security personnel per 1,000 inhabitants." Since the force-to-population ratio is based on the presumption that the intervening power is the principal counterinsurgency force, this ratio is not particularly helpful for identifying or analyzing special warfare campaigns. Special warfare FID, as defined here, is not simply an underresourced form of counterinsurgency; rather it is a distinct operational concept. Regarding the size of the U.S. global military presence, see Michael J. Lostumbo, Michael J. McNerney, Eric Peltz, Derek Eaton, David R. Frelinger, Victoria A. Greenfield, John Halliday, Patrick Mills, Bruce R. Nardulli, Stacie L. Pettyjohn, Jerry M. Sollinger, and Stephen Worman, *Overseas Basing of U.S. Military Forces: An Assessment of Relative Costs and Strategic Benefits*, Santa Monica, Calif.: RAND Corporation, RR-201-OSD, 2013.

ued to execute important missions.[39] Covert or clandestine missions will typically have an even smaller presence or, in some cases, none at all in the targeted country.[40] The number of CIA personnel (including seconded military) involved in both unconventional warfare and FID operations in Laos was limited by the U.S. ambassador to "a few hundred, many of them stationed in nearby Thailand."[41] Prior to the Falkland Islands war, Argentina acted as a proxy for U.S. unconventional warfare operations in Nicaragua, providing trainers and combat advisers to the Contras.[42] This "small-footprint" characteristic does not preclude conventional force participation (e.g., via the Army's Regionally Aligned Forces), or even a lead role in a special warfare campaigns.[43] Rather, it is a direct consequence of special warfare as an indirect approach prioritizing working through partners to satisfy broader strategic or environmental constraints (e.g., to avoid escalating tensions with a neighboring peer competitor) or to set the conditions for longer-term success (such as limiting partner dependency). Signature management becomes far more sensitive, covert or not, because large footprints leave little question about a partner's relationship with the United States. The local partner's preference regarding the disclosure of its relationship with the United States will likely be driven by a the sources of its own legitimacy and credibility.

That special warfare campaigns are protracted, sometimes requiring extensive preparation and patience, is a recurrent theme in the lit-

---

[39] Watts et al., 2012; David C. Palilonis, *Operation Enduring Freedom—Philippines: A Demonstration of Economy of Force*, Newport, R.I.: U.S. Naval War College, May 2009.

[40] Interview by the research team, May 21, 2013.

[41] Douglas S. Blaufarb, *Organizing and Managing Unconventional War in Laos, 1962–1970*, Santa Monica, Calif.: RAND Corporation, R-919-ARPA, January 1972.

[42] Ryan C. Agee and Maurice K. DuClos, *Why UW: Factoring in the Decision Point for Unconventional Warfare*, thesis, Monterey, Calif.: Naval Postgraduate School, December 2012.

[43] Antonieta Rico, "New Training to Focus on Regionally Aligned Forces Concept," *Defense News*, October 23, 2013.

erature and in practitioners' statements.[44] The special warfare efforts in our data set lasted an average of more than nine years (see Appendix D in the companion volume). One interviewee noted that special warfare is "more like fighting crime domestically than decisive operations."[45] Large-footprint interventions, including counterinsurgency operations, are typically intended to be short term because of the cost and time involved, though mission creep and credibility risk frequently increase the duration incrementally. FID and unconventional warfare are both relatively low-cost in materiel terms and so can realistically be sustained for longer time horizons. Policymakers still do not like committing to indefinite investments, so obstacles to long-term planning still exist. The duration of these conflicts places a greater premium on campaign continuity across changes in command and unit rotations (also see Appendix B in the companion volume).[46]

Special warfare often requires intensive interagency cooperation. SOF conducting special warfare might find themselves supporting conventional forces, DoS, or the CIA and will almost always work with them. During noncrisis operations, DoD activities in country will typically be conducted at the direction of the chief of mission. In covert unconventional warfare operations, dependency on interagency partners for success will be heightened by the historical propensity to place the CIA in the lead, though this is at the discretion of the President rather than a statutory requirement. Although DoD has developed much greater interagency experience over the past decade, much of it has been in places where DoD has controlled the lion's share of resources and influence. Special warfare campaigns in which DoD is the junior partner in an interagency effort will entail a greater burden to collaborate effectively.

Significantly, Watts et al. have found that "minimalist stabilization" efforts (roughly corresponding to our definition of FID) are

---

[44] Rupert Smith, *The Utility of Force: The Art of War in the Modern World*, New York: Alfred A. Knopf, 2005.

[45] Interview by the research team, May 16, 2013.

[46] Interview by the research team, December 13, 2013.

frequently able to stave off a partner nation's defeat—protracting the conflict—but not secure victory for two reasons:

> First, although it can strengthen host-nation security forces, it seldom is capable of transforming them into highly effective counterinsurgents due to the weaknesses of host nations' governments. Second, minimalist stabilization provides few capabilities with which to significantly improve the governance of host nations.[47]

These weaknesses, identified even in ultimately successful historical FID efforts,[48] highlight the importance of employing a whole-of-government approach that addresses more than the tactical efficacy of the partner force but also looks more holistically at institutional reform and other systemic challenges.

For additional study of special warfare, we encourage practitioners and analysts to read the *Assessing Revolutionary and Insurgent Strategies* series, which contains a rich set of case studies and analyses of special warfare themes.[49]

---

[47] Watts et al., 2012, p. 83.

[48] See Dobbins et al., 2013.

[49] Paul J. Tompkins, Jr., ed., *Assessing Revolutionary and Insurgent Strategies: Casebook on Insurgency and Revolutionary Warfare, Volume I: 1933–1962*, rev. ed., Ft. Bragg, N.C.: U.S. Army Special Operations Command and Johns Hopkins University Applied Physics Laboratory National Security Analysis Department, January 25, 2013; Paul J. Tompkins, Jr., and Chuck Crossett, eds., *Assessing Revolutionary and Insurgent Strategies: Casebook on Insurgency and Revolutionary Warfare, Volume II: 1962–2009*, Ft. Bragg, N.C.: U.S. Army Special Operations Command and Johns Hopkins University Applied Physics Laboratory National Security Analysis Department, April 27, 2012; Paul J. Tompkins, Jr., and Nathan Bos, ed., *Assessing Revolutionary and Insurgent Strategies: Human Factor Considerations of Undergrounds in Insurgencies*, Ft. Bragg, N.C.: U.S. Army Special Operations Command and Johns Hopkins University Applied Physics Laboratory National Security Analysis Department, January 25, 2013; Paul J. Tompkins, Jr., and Robert Leonhard, eds., *Assessing Revolutionary and Insurgent Strategies: Underground in Insurgent, Revolutionary, and Resistance Warfare*, 2nd ed., Ft. Bragg, N.C.: U.S. Army Special Operations Command and Johns Hopkins University Applied Physics Laboratory National Security Analysis Department, January 25, 2013; Paul J. Tompkins, Jr., and Summer Newtown, eds., *Assessing Revolutionary and Insurgent Strategies: Irregular Warfare Annotated Bibliography*, Ft. Bragg, N.C.: U.S. Army Special

Advantages and Risks of Special Warfare

Special warfare has particular relevance to the current global security environment as policymakers seek options short of large-scale intervention to manage (or assist in managing) challenges both acute (e.g., Syrian civil war, Ukraine crisis) and chronic (e.g., insurgency in the Philippines). Special warfare campaigns offer several advantages in furthering U.S. interests by providing options to meet these challenges. Educating policymakers and key elements of U.S. national security agencies about SOF capabilities in special warfare is important for managing continued U.S. international commitments in an era of declining resources.

Strategic Advantages

Some advantages of special warfare approaches are as follows:[50]

- *Improved understanding and shaping of the environment.* Special warfare, executed through intelligence or selected military activities, can improve contextual understanding of potential partners and "ground truth" before the United States commits to a course of action. As the operating environment is better understood, stakeholders can be engaged, their compatibility with U.S. interests assessed, and their capability selectively augmented. What the SOF community refers to as PE activities are thought by special warfare practitioners to be key to achieving these effects.[51]

Operations Command and Johns Hopkins University Applied Physics Laboratory National Security Analysis Department, June 2, 2011.

[50] For a broader discussion of SOF in a strategic context, see Colin S. Gray, *Explorations in Strategy*, Westport, Conn.: Praeger, 1998; Lucien S. Vandenbroucke, *Perilous Options: Special Operations as an Instrument of U.S. Foreign Policy*, New York: Oxford University Press, 1993; James D. Kiras, *Special Operations and Strategy: From World War II to the War on Terrorism*, New York: Routledge, 2006; and Joseph D. Celeski, Timothy S. Slemp, and John D. Jogerst, *An Introduction to Special Operations Power: Origins, Concepts and Application*, unpublished manuscript, 2013.

[51] An ambassador may understandably have some anxiety over what impact the disclosure of PE being conducted might have on diplomatic relations with the targeted country. See the points on policy fratricide and disclosure in the next section, "Limits and Risks." For report-

- *Cost-imposing strategies.* Special warfare's small-footprint approach allows the United States to pursue cost-imposing strategies that force opponents to spend disproportionate resources to defend against friendly capabilities. The United States has been on the wrong end of the cost-exchange equation in recent years (e.g., counterinsurgency to deny al Qaeda sanctuary), and special warfare can help reverse this.
- *Managed escalation and credibility risk.* Given a decision to intervene, policymakers could use special warfare to avoid making commitments beyond U.S. interests. However, it will be important to carefully assess the escalation criteria and options of adversaries and their external partners. Assessment of the adversary's (and the United States') likely escalation behavior is fraught with uncertainty, not least because adversaries may not understand how their own preferences may change as the situation evolves (e.g., responses to jingoistic pressure from domestic constituencies).[52]

---

ing on U.S. preparation of the environment activities, see Mark Mazzetti, *The Way of the Knife: The CIA, a Secret Army, and a War at the Ends of the Earth*, New York: Penguin Books, 2013.

[52] The notion that special warfare campaigns' escalation dynamics are simpler to manage than those of conventional or distant-strike campaigns is context-dependent, but we offer the following evidence and arguments. Distant-strike campaigns against a peer competitor suffer from a crisis instability problem, in which each side has an incentive to strike first, and an ambiguity problem in which a lack of U.S. knowledge over the disposition of strategic weapons (such as mobile nuclear ballistic missiles) may cause the targeted state to believe the United States is escalating vertically beyond what is intended. Since special warfare campaigns unfold over a protracted time horizon, the same crisis instability problem does not hold. Conventional campaigns (here, either major combat or counterinsurgency operations) suffer from much larger political sunk costs that create incentives to "gamble for resurrection," a phrase used to describe President Lyndon Johnson's decision to escalate in Vietnam. See George W. Downs and David M. Rocke, "Conflict, Agency, and Gambling for Resurrection: The Principal-Agent Problem Goes to War," *American Journal of Political Science*, Vol. 38, No. 2, May 1994.

Empirically, analysis of our data set of special warfare campaigns found most outcomes "indeterminate," meaning neither a decisive win nor loss at the operational level, and yet only in the case of South Vietnam did U.S. policymakers escalate the conflict into a "conventional" war. In the 1980s, Congress actually passed a law shutting down U.S. support to the Contras in Nicaragua, indicating the different political dynamics governing special warfare campaigns and unpopular conventional wars. In the latter, efforts in Congress to

- *Sustainable solutions.* Sustainability has two components—fiscal and political. Special warfare's small-footprint approach can be more fiscally and politically sustainable than alternatives when underlying sources of conflict cannot be resolved in the short term, preserving core U.S. interests at costs that the nation is willing to bear. From a host-nation or coalition political perspective, commanders can also use special warfare's partner-centric approach to design campaigns around a partner's core interests, rather than hoping to transform them in ways that have frequently proven to be ephemeral.

Limits and Risks

As noted earlier, special warfare campaigns are characterized by operations in which the local partner provides the main effort. As one practitioner noted, "In special warfare you're the navigator, not the driver."[53] This dependency on partners carries a set of risks and limitations, as do other characteristics of special warfare. The following are some examples:

- *Divergent partner objectives.* A partner may have core objectives that conflict with those of the United States, or it may simply prioritize them differently. Assessments before and during campaigns are necessary to ensure that the partnership remains appropriate vehicle for advancing U.S. policy goals. U.S. policymakers need to be prepared to terminate efforts if partner objectives diverge too much from U.S. objectives. This is simpler to do in a special warfare campaign than in a conventional one, though it is still not easy.
- *Ineffective partner capability.* The opponent's level of capability and operational tempo relative to the partner's may render special warfare solutions ineffective within the required time horizon.

---

halt funding for the conflict frequently become conflated with the emotive issue of support for U.S. troops (e.g., Operation Iraqi Freedom). Conversely, a U.S. unconventional warfare campaign supporting Tibet lasted decades without serious escalation risk or domestic political contestation.

[53] Interview with Paul Tompkins, Ft. Benning, Ga., October 23, 2013.

If U.S. strategic objectives include regime change within a few months but the prospective partner's guerrilla capability requires a year to mature, unconventional warfare may be more appropriate as a supporting effort to a conventional campaign rather than as the campaign's main effort. Appropriate peacetime shaping efforts (e.g., building partner capacity) can help mitigate this risk.

- *Unacceptable partner behavior.* Some partners may behave in ways that transgress U.S. normative standards (e.g., respect for human rights) and undermine their own sources of legitimacy. These risks can be mitigated through monitoring, screening, and institutional reform but should also be weighed against the policy goals driving the intervention.

- *Policy fratricide.* If special warfare campaigns are not carefully integrated into a holistic U.S. policy toward the targeted country, U.S. efforts can either come into direct conflict or fall out of balance. As an example, disproportionate resourcing of military capacity building might undermine longer-term democratization efforts by making the military the only credible institution in a state where the United States is conducting a FID campaign (e.g., Panama in the 1980s) or in a third country through which the United States is resourcing an unconventional warfare effort (e.g., growth of Pakistan's Inter-Services Intelligence directorate in the 1980s). Even if efforts are well integrated to support a unified national policy for the targeted country, the exposure of covert activities might lead to inadvertent escalation with another state, or it could degrade perceptions of U.S. respect for national sovereignty among key population segments (e.g., the Arab "street"). Successful special warfare campaigns are built on a foundation of thorough coordination among the combatant command, country team, and National Security Council staff.

- *Disclosure.* The global proliferation of information technology erodes the ability to keep covert activities covert.[54] This prolifera-

---

[54] Although the proliferation of information technology has made keeping operations clandestine or covert more challenging, in other ways, it enables new opportunities to exercise influence activities, bringing about a more nuanced appreciation of the operating environment.

tion enhances the risk of disclosure through the digital footprint of prospective covert operators (e.g., Facebook history); third parties (e.g., Sohaib Athar's tweets during the raid on Osama bin Laden's compound, crowdsourced analysis of YouTube videos in conflict areas); and the capabilities of targeted states (e.g., biometric surveillance). A variety of tactical and technical behaviors and investments can be adopted to partially mitigate these risks.

Although the United States might avoid some of these risks by acting unilaterally, it would lose the strategic advantages identified here.

CHAPTER THREE

Operational Art in Special Warfare

This chapter presents the conceptual foundation for understanding and applying operational art in special warfare. It begins with a discussion of the current joint definition of operational art, followed by a brief overview of the origins of operational art and a discussion of its modern elements. It then explains how those elements must be understood and applied in the context of special warfare campaigns and offers a theory of operational art for achieving strategic objectives in special warfare. In Chapter Five, we present two case studies of special warfare to test the theory.

Despite Clausewitz's admonition that "war is not merely an act of policy, but a true political instrument," much of the literature surrounding operational art creates the impression that it is an autonomous military space, with military professionals receiving policy objectives from an equally distinct political sphere and proceeding with the task of campaign planning.[1] The campaign is then executed without subsequent intervention by policymakers, unless their objectives change. In practice, the formulation of campaigns, a critical output of operational art, involves a strategic dialogue between the theater commander and policymakers, through which ends, ways, and means are gradually brought into alignment. As policymakers come to a clearer understanding of the costs of particular objectives, and as the military commander comes to a clearer understanding of what objectives policymakers are seeking, each actor is likely to make important adjust-

---

[1] Clausewitz, 1984; Justin Kelly and Mike Brennan, *Alien: How Operational Art Devoured Strategy*, Carlisle, Pa.: Strategic Studies Institute, Army War College, September 2009.

ments. At times, the distinction between the role of the policymaker as a source of guidance and the role of the policymaker as an actor capable of directly affecting events will break down. Key policymakers have legal authorities and political power, enabling them to take actions that the military alone cannot (e.g., to credibly negotiate, rally domestic support, or enforce unity of effort among U.S. government agencies). The "unequal" civil-military dialogue—unequal because policymakers have final authority—is important not only for ensuring that campaign plans reflect policy goals but also as an occasion for policymakers' to refine their strategy, on which hangs the ultimate meaning of the campaign.[2] Chapter Four provides a more detailed discussion of the formal process of this civil-military dialogue in the context of the Joint Strategic Planning System.

Defining Operational Art

The current joint definition of operational art does not add up to a clear and coherent concept: "The cognitive approach by commanders and staffs—supported by their skill, knowledge, experience, creativity, and judgment—to develop strategies, campaigns, and operations to organize and employ military forces by integrating ends, ways, and means."[3] It is simultaneously something *cognitive*, involving personal knowledge, skills, and attributes, such as creativity; something *strategic*, involving ends, ways, and means; and something *operational*, involving the organization and employment of military forces. The Army's definition is on the right track but focuses primarily on traditional uses of force: "Operational art is the pursuit of strategic objectives, in whole or in part, through the arrangement of tactical actions in time, space,

---

[2] Samuel P. Huntington, *The Soldier and the State: The Theory and Politics of Civil-Military Relations.* Cambridge, Mass.: Harvard University Press, 1985; Eliot A. Cohen, *Supreme Command: Soldiers, Statesmen, and Leadership in Wartime*, New York: Anchor Books, 2003; Bob Woodward, *Obama's Wars*, New York: Simon and Schuster, 2010. In Woodward, see the discussion of military advice provided to President Obama prior to his adoption of the Afghanistan counterinsurgency strategy articulated in his 2009 West Point speech.

[3] U.S. Joint Chiefs of Staff, 2015.

and purpose."[4] This links tactical actions to strategic objectives, but *the arrangement of tactical actions in time, space, and purpose* describes good tactics, or perhaps grand tactics, but not operational art.

To gain a clear concept of operational art, it is helpful to contrast current doctrine with the 1986 version of FM 100-5, *Operations*. While it focused exclusively on conventional campaigns, the final articulation of AirLand Battle clarifies the concepts and ideas. *War* is a "national undertaking that must be coordinated from the highest levels of policymaking to the basic levels of execution." *Military strategy* is "the art and science of employing the armed forces of a nation or alliance to secure policy objectives by the application or threat of force." *Operational art* is "the employment of military forces to attain strategic goals in a theater of war through the design, organization and conduct of campaigns and major operations." It continues,

> Reduced to its essentials, operational art requires the combatant commander to answer three questions:
>
> 1. What military condition must be produced to achieve the strategic goal?
> 2. What sequence of actions is most likely to produce that outcome?
> 3. How should military resources be applied to accomplish that sequence of actions?[5]

The *essence of operational art* is "the identification of the enemy's center of gravity—his source of strength—and the concentration of superior combat power against that point to achieve a decisive success."[6] To relate this idea back to the three essential questions, military resources must be applied at decisive points through a sufficient sequence of actions to defeat the enemy strength that resists the desired outcome. A *campaign* is "a series of joint actions designed to attain a strategic objective in a theater of war"; there may be simulta-

---

[4] Headquarters, U.S. Department of the Army, 2012b, p. 9.

[5] Headquarters, U.S. Department of the Army, 1986, pp. 9–10.

[6] Headquarters, U.S. Department of the Army, 1986, p. 10.

neous or sequential campaigns, depending on the situation. "While operational art sets the objectives and pattern of military activities," *tactics* is the art of translating "combat power into victorious battles and engagements."[7] Thus, the 1986 version of FM 100-5, *Operations,* provides a clear conceptual framework for defining operational art and integrating military activity from national policymaking to small-unit actions—in conventional warfare.

The "center-of-gravity" concept is well known but not known well. Robust discussion within the military continues to surround what, precisely, the center of gravity is and what role it should play in campaign design. Some critics have suggested that the term be dropped from the joint lexicon.[8] The objective of operational art is clearly to conduct campaigns that achieve strategic objectives, but it is desirable to provide commanders with conceptual tools that will assist them in identifying how to do that. The research team was faced with the choice of either to develop a new conceptual tool to aid commanders or to attempt to introduce clarity to an existing concept that has been a source of controversy and confusion. We chose the latter course of action. We have tried to address this controversy by providing a clear description of what *center of gravity* is and how it may be identified in the section "Elements of Operational Design and Special Warfare," later in this chapter. We also provide examples of the center of gravity in special warfare campaigns through case studies and notional scenarios.

Ever since General Gordon Sullivan wrote about the expansion of "war in the information age," the intellectual challenge facing the U.S. Army has been to define a clear conceptual framework that incorporates multiple forms of operational art:

> We will no longer be able to understand war simply as the armies
> of one nation-state fighting another. This definition is too narrow.
> Nation-states do not have a monopoly on war making; a variety
> of entities can wage war—corporations, religious groups, terror-

---

[7]   Headquarters, U.S. Department of the Army, 1986, p. 10.

[8]   Celestino Perez, ed., *Addressing the Fog of COG: Perspective on the Center of Gravity in U.S. Military Doctrine*, Ft. Leavenworth, Kan.: Combat Studies Institute Press, 2012.

ists, tribes, guerrilla bands, drug cartels, crime syndicates, and clans. The net result is a blurring of the distinction between war and operations other than war.[9]

The challenge is defining the overarching principles in a unified framework that guides each form of operational art while preserving its unique tenets. To use an analogy, the form of operational art may be a "classical Rembrandt," conventional campaigns against a state's military forces (e.g., the Napoleonic wars, World War II, AirLand Battle, Operation Desert Storm). It may be a "modern Picasso," irregular campaigns against nonstate actors (e.g., the conflicts in the Philippines and Malaya, Afghanistan in the 1980s, contingencies in Iraq after the fall of Saddam Hussein). It may be an "impressionist Renoir," hybrid campaigns against mixed threats (e.g., the Vietnam War). It may even resemble "Michelangelo's sculpture" when policymakers use force as a finely tuned instrument in a coercion campaign designed to make the costs of resistance gradually greater than the costs of yielding a limited strategic objective (e.g., Kosovo, Libya). Although some strategists have described the modern operational art forms as "winning ugly," their "beauty" is in the eye of policymakers who successfully achieve their strategic objectives.[10] The purpose of this analysis is to answer these questions: *What common principles make these art forms successful? What differences make each art form a unique expression?*

It is no longer sufficient for operational commanders and planners, in a combatant or service component command, to be proficient in only one form of operational art. They must have expertise in all forms of operational art if they are to design successful campaigns across the full range of military operations in modern conflicts. Failing to understand the nature of a conflict and planning for one type of campaign when quite a different type is called for will lead to problems, as the U.S. Army discovered after it seized Baghdad in 2003.[11]

---

[9] Gordon Sullivan, "War in the Information Age," *Military Review*, Vol. 74, No. 4, April 1994, p. 54.

[10] Daalder and O'Hanlon, 2000.

[11] See Echevarria, 2011, pp. 137–165.

Origins of Operational Art

The evolution of operational art has been driven by several key factors. First, grand strategy may demand new operational concepts to counter new and different threats to a state's national security interests.[12] Second, a change in capabilities may affect how generals design campaigns to make effective use of tactical engagements and achieve strategic objectives.[13] Third, enemy adaptation—either matching the operational innovation in symmetrical terms or choosing an asymmetric response to negate its advantages—requires the Army to be a learning organization that practices continuous innovation rather than stagnating comfortably, resting on past successes.

From Alexander to Frederick, the art of war had two levels: Strategy brought armies to the point of accepting battle, and tactics determined how those battles were fought. Winning decisive battles at Marathon, Syracuse, Gaugamela, Carthage, Hastings, Orleans, Blenheim, and Leuthen was sufficient to win the war, or at least to extract a concession and gain a temporary armistice in the enduring pursuit of power.

It was not until the Napoleonic wars that the operational level of war began to emerge as the "gray area" between strategy and tactics. Napoleon brought about a revolution in military affairs by harnessing the power of nationalism and the modern state to extend war in the physical and human domains. Instead of conscripted or mercenary soldiers who fought because they feared being disciplined more than they feared the enemy, Napoleon enlisted Frenchmen who also fought for their country. Consequently, he raised larger armies and suffered less from desertion. Freed from the logistical tether of short supply lines to fixed bases, Napoleon's marshals conducted distributed, corps-level operational maneuver over larger areas. By selecting leaders based on

---

[12] James McDonough, "The Operational Art: Quo Vadis?" in Richard Hooker, Jr., ed., *Maneuver Warfare Anthology*, Novato, Calif.: Presidio Press, 1993, p. 106.

[13] See Michael Krause and Cody Phillips, *Historical Perspectives of the Operational Art*, Ft. McNair, Washington, D.C.: U.S. Army Center of Military History, 2005, and MacGregor Knox and Williamson Murray, *The Dynamics of Military Revolution 1300–2050*, New York: Cambridge University Press, 2009.

a merit-based system, the corps moved independently yet still concentrated at the decisive time and place to win battles.

After several catastrophic defeats, the allies implemented the reforms necessary to match Napoleon. Consequently, wars no longer ended with a single "decisive battle," though generals were slow to realize this point. The Russians lost at Borodino and Moscow but kept fighting to drive the French out of their country with help from "General Winter." Passing the *culminating point* of the offensive, Napoleon lost an army in Russia in 1812, raised another army in Germany only to lose again at Leipzig in 1813, and raised yet another army to defend France in 1814. Thus, the allies were forced to design sequential campaigns to defeat the French operational and strategic *centers of gravity*—the French army and Paris—to achieve their *end-state conditions* that would restore the balance of power in Europe. These campaigns were based on geographic *lines of operation* that connected the force to the enemy through a series of *decisive points* that offered an opportunity to engage the enemy on favorable terms.

Competitive refinement and innovation have continued to characterize the history of operational art. Through the American civil war and Prussian wars with France and Austria, the concept of annihilation evolved under the impact of rail, telegraph, mass production, nationalism, and other factors that made discrete battles less decisive. During World War II, Germany successfully exploited the mechanization revolution through maneuver warfare, while Russia developed a superior concept of "deep operations theory," and the United States began to exploit the opportunities of joint operations through naval and aviation maneuver and firepower in support of land operations. The introduction of nuclear weapons drove the superpowers away from direct conflict and into proxy wars, in such places as Vietnam and Afghanistan, where new unconventional warfare and counterinsurgency concepts were developed and employed. The post-Vietnam focus on the defense of Europe led the U.S. Army to develop the AirLand Battle concept to disrupt successive of echelons of Russian armor, enabling the piecemeal defeat of Russian forces in the close battle. The success of U.S. forces in Operation Desert Storm spurred interest in an information revolution in military affairs, optimistically thought to have dissipated the fog of war. Post–Cold War peacekeeping operations elicited new interest in "military operations other than war," and U.S. doctrine was updated with such concepts as "legitimacy" and "restraint." By 2001, in the wake of the intervention in Kosovo, U.S. doctrine included the concept of "full-spectrum" operations, recognizing that offensive, defensive, stability, and support tasks may be undertaken simultaneously throughout campaigns.

One of the more famous campaigns in recent history focused on irregular threats. General Petraeus chose to name his operational design in Iraq "Anaconda," echoing Winfield Scott's campaign plan to defeat the South and illustrating how he sought to apply concentric pressure along multiple lines of effort to isolate, divide, and defeat the enemy's center of gravity—the alliance among al Qaeda in Iraq, the Sunni insurgency, and other militant groups. To be sure, the functional lines of effort included strengthening and working with partners. But, ultimately, the joint civil-military campaign plan succeeded in reducing levels of violence because it was successfully oriented on the enemy's center of gravity. Figure 3.1 illustrates this structure.

While the Americans were engaged in Afghanistan and Iraq, the Israelis discovered that Hezbollah had developed a new form of operational art. Or, perhaps more accurately, Hezbollah combined elements of different art forms in a hybrid model and benefited from skillful media exploitation of Israeli mistakes. At the strategic level, Hezbollah was a state within a state that made defense policy and offered basic services to gain and maintain the support of the Shi'a population. At the operational level, Hezbollah had both irregular guerrillas and a form of conventional militias. At the tactical level, it defended complex terrain in depth, with obstacles covered by fire, including antitank missiles and mortars. Yet, its form of operational art relied on the effective use of information operations to appeal to Muslims while simultaneously degrading popular support for Israel. [14] Meanwhile, the Israelis embraced a complicated form of systemic operational design, a type of general system theory akin to the U.S. version of effects-based opera-

---

[14] See Andrew Exum, *Hizballah at War: A Military Assessment*, Policy Focus No. 63, Washington, D.C.: Washington Institute for Near East Policy, December 2006.

Figure 3.1
Anaconda Operational Design in Iraq

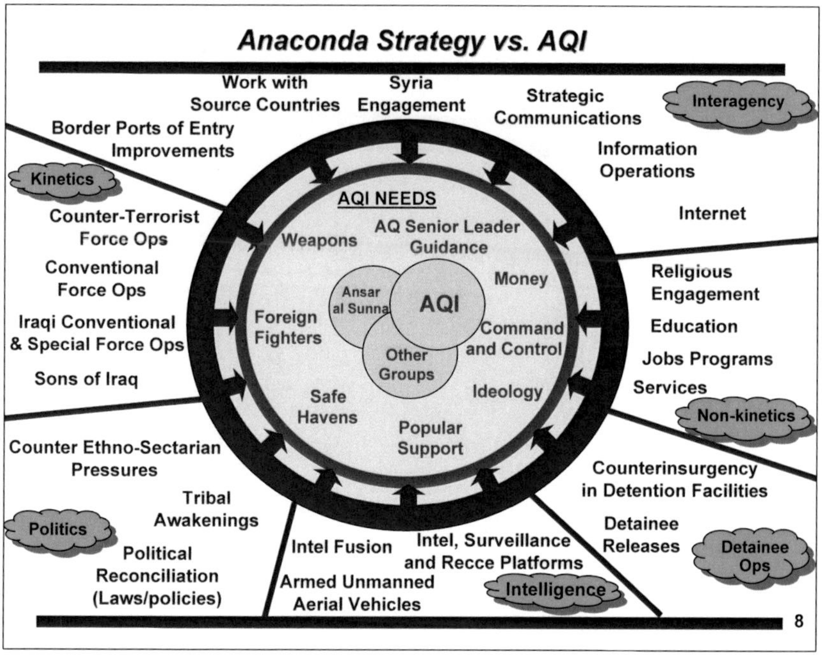

Anaconda Strategy vs. AQI

Work with Source Countries
Syria Engagement
Strategic Communications
Interagency
Border Ports of Entry Improvements
Kinetics
Information Operations
Counter-Terrorist Force Ops
Internet
Conventional Force Ops
Iraqi Conventional & Special Force Ops
Sons of Iraq
Counter Ethno-Sectarian Pressures
Tribal Awakenings
Politics
Political Reconciliation (Laws/policies)
Intel Fusion
Armed Unmanned Aerial Vehicles
Intel, Surveillance and Recce Platforms
Intelligence
Detainee Releases
Detainee Ops
Counterinsurgency in Detention Facilities
Non-kinetics
Services
Jobs Programs
Education
Religious Engagement

AQI NEEDS
Weapons
AQ Senior Leader Guidance
Money
Foreign Fighters
Ansar al Sunna
AQI
Other Groups
Command and Control
Safe Havens
Popular Support
Ideology

8

SOURCE: David H. Petraeus, "Multi-National Forces Iraq: Charts to Accompany the Testimony of GEN David H. Petraeus," PowerPoint slides, April 8–9, 2008, slide 8.
NOTE: AQI = al Qaeda in Iraq.
RAND RR779-3.1

tions that most Israeli officers did not understand and that ultimately degraded their operational efficacy.

From Classic Operational Art to Special Warfare

Operational art has evolved over time, driven by the demands of strategy, revolutionary new capabilities, and the need to continuously learn and adapt to changing threats (see Appendix A in the companion volume). The modern conceptual framework of operational art must be broad enough to include forms of conventional, irregular, hybrid, and coercion campaigns but specific enough to offer operational commanders and planners a useful tool to design effective campaigns. While the joint definition of *operational art* leaves much to be desired, joint doctrine includes classical principles and elements of operational design that could meet this universal test, if properly defined. The purpose of this section is to define a modern framework for operational art for subsequent examination and application to special warfare.

Before designing campaigns, the operational-level commander must first understand the unique nature of the conflict.[15] Understanding the war is an essential task because it leads to the appropriate political-military relationship, military aim, and amount of effort. Wars are lost when policymakers and commanders fail to establish effective relationships between the levels of war because they do not understand themselves, their enemy, or their unique war. To understand the nature of the war, one must understand the forces that define it.

Clausewitz described the political objective as the "essential factor in the equation" that determines the intensity of the war: "The smaller the penalty you demand from your opponent, the less you can expect him to try and deny it to you; the smaller the effort he makes, the less you need make yourself." If reason rules war, then "the political objective—the original motive for the war—will thus determine both the military objective to be reached and the amount of effort it requires."[16] Yet, Clausewitz also recognized that extreme forces were a function of violence and passion:

> The political object cannot, however, *in itself* provide the standard of measurement. . . . The same political object can elicit *differing* reactions from different peoples, and even from the same people at different times. We can therefore take the political object as

---

[15] Specifically, according to Clausewitz,

The first, the supreme, the most far-reaching act of judgment that the statesman and commander have to make is to establish by that test the kind of war on which they are embarking; neither mistaking it for, nor trying to turn it into, something alien to its nature. This is the first of all strategic questions and the most comprehensive. (Clausewitz, 1984, p. 88)

[16] Clausewitz, 1984, p. 81.

a standard only if we think of *the influence it can exert upon the forces it is meant to move.*[17]

Because cultural, moral, and psychological factors determine the complex relationship between reason and passion, Clausewitz introduced a third force that defines the nature of war: the exercise of creative art within the realm of chance and probability. Because uncertainty is inherent in war, campaign plans are essentially theories based on assumptions ruled by chance and probability: "In short, absolute, so-called mathematical, factors never find a firm basis in military calculations. From the very start there is an interplay of possibilities, probabilities, good luck and bad that weaves its way throughout the length and breadth of the tapestry."[18]

In sum, Clausewitz developed three realistic, dynamic, and variable forces to define war—reason, violence, and chance. Reason guides war by determining the ends. Violence sustains war by motivating the means (i.e., passions). Chance and creativity drive plans for war and define the ways. Each force in each war is different; each force in the same war may change. Leaders begin the synthesis process by defining their own political objectives, assessing the value of those objectives to the enemy, and determining the enemy's will to fight. Based on their estimates of reason and passion (both their own and their adversary's), leaders determine the aim and employment of military force. As a generalization, if the enemy is fighting to defend interests that the people believe are truly vital, then the required force would lead to the first type of war: Destroy the enemy's armed forces and dictate the terms for peace. Less-than-vital interests or significant resistance would lead to the second type of war: Seize a bargaining advantage to negotiate peace.

The "trinitarian" framework for understanding the nature of the war is suitable in both conventional and irregular conflicts, but the difference between the political and military objectives can be critical. For example, in World War II, the political objectives were the

---

[17] Clausewitz, 1984, p. 81; emphasis in original.

[18] Clausewitz, 1984, p. 81.

unconditional surrender of Germany and Japan, followed by political reconstruction. The supporting military objective was the defeat of the military forces that offered resistance. The operational cause and strategic effect relationship is clear: Military defeat leads to political defeat. In contrast, the political objective in Iraq was a representative government, at peace with its neighbors and a partner in the war on terrorism. The military objectives were to secure the environment and support an interagency process to build national institutions. The operational cause and strategic effect relationship was less clear: How does tactical security lead to political stability when so many other variables are involved? That is why special warfare's employment of influence in the human domain to achieve political objectives—mobilization, neutralization, integration—is so vital to successful campaigns.

Elements of Operational Design and Special Warfare

The elements of operational art provide the "connective tissue" between tactical actions and strategic objectives by supporting the design of successful campaigns. The following definitions and illustrative examples focus on the elements of operational design, combining ideas from joint and Army doctrine with the conceptual framework proposed by Joe Strange.[19] We use the Army's elements of design, since the joint doctrine still seems burdened by the language of effects-based operations.[20] For each element, we identify special warfare–unique characteristics (see Figure 3.2 and the discussion that follows).

---

[19] Doctrinal sources are JP 1-02 (U.S. Joint Chiefs of Staff, 2015); JP 3-0 (U.S. Joint Chiefs of Staff, 2011b); JP 5-0 (U.S. Joint Chiefs of Staff, *Joint Operation Planning*, Joint Publication 5-0, Washington, D.C., August 11, 2011a); Army Doctrinal Reference Publication 3-0 (Headquarters, U.S. Department of the Army, 2012b); Army Doctrinal Reference Publication 5-0 (Headquarters, U.S. Department of the Army, *The Operations Process*, Army Doctrinal Reference Publication 5-0, May 2012a). See also Joe Strange, "Centers of Gravity and Critical Vulnerabilities: Building on the Clausewitzian Foundation So That We May All Speak the Same Language," *Perspectives on Warfighting*, No. 4, 2nd ed., Quantico, Va.: Marine Corps War College, 1996.

[20] For a critique of effects-based operations in doctrine, see Ben Connable, *Embracing the Fog of War: Assessment and Metrics in Counterinsurgency*, Santa Monica, Calif.: RAND Corporation, MG-1086-DOD, 2012.

Figure 3.2
Elements of Operational Design and Their Role

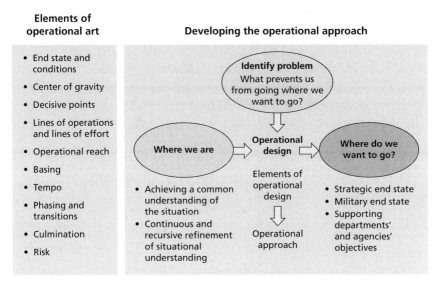

SOURCES: Headquarters, U.S. Department of the Army, 2012a; U.S. Joint Chiefs of Staff, 2011a, p. III-3, Figure III-2.
RAND RR779-3.2

End State and Conditions

The end state consists of the conditions that the commander wants to exist when the operation ends. A clearly defined end state minimizes risk and promotes unity of effort, joint and interagency synchronization, and the disciplined use of initiative.

In conventional conflicts, end states from the tactical to the strategic level are typically defined in military terms. In special warfare, end states may be purely military (e.g., unconventional warfare operations with the *peshmerga* to secure northern Iraq in 2003), but they also may encompass more directly *political* end states. The United States may have a policy objective that goes beyond regime change, such as preferences about the composition of the postconflict regime (as in Iran in 1953).

In special warfare, legitimacy is sometimes identified as "the main objective."[21] Legitimacy is a quality ascribed to belligerents by the population, implying consensual support rather than coerced support. Since coercing support requires substantially more effort than attracting consensual support, legitimacy plays a powerful role in special warfare, setting the conditions for sustainable solutions. Insurgents and state forces have different sources of legitimacy and may be faced with different burdens in achieving it.[22] In counterinsurgency campaigns in which the United States takes the lead in providing security, command efforts are sometimes split between increasing the legitimacy of U.S. forces and increasing the legitimacy of the host-nation government. In special warfare, there may be efforts to reduce the population's hostility toward the United States, but the focus is typically on the legitimacy of the partner's force.

Center of Gravity

Center of gravity is the source of power that provides moral or physical strength, freedom of action, or will to act. At the strategic level, this is best conceptualized as the source of (moral) will to implement the policy being pursued through the conflict. At the operational level, it should be understood as the entity through which the strategic center of gravity is principally exercised (e.g., the possessor of critical capabilities).

The friendly operational center of gravity in conventional conflicts is often some element of U.S. forces. In special warfare, it will typically be a partner's force. In many special warfare cases, the United States, through SOF or other government agencies, will have to construct the operational center of gravity. This might involve training to increase the professionalism of an existent force, but it may extend to the mobilization of the population. The mobilization of a population and its

---

[21] Headquarters, U.S. Department of the Army, and Headquarters, U.S. Marine Corps, 2014, p. 1-19.

[22] For example, the fundamental attribution error associated with ingroup-outgroup dynamics (Jason Lyall, Graeme Blair, and Kosuke Imai, "Explaining Support for Combatants During Wartime: A Survey Experiment in Afghanistan," *American Political Science Review*, Vol. 107, No. 4, November 2013).

transformation into an instrument of policy, whether through induction into the military or through protest movements, has largely been lost from conventional operational art because the role of military and civilian leadership in the United States has been sufficiently differentiated so that the political mobilization of the people (the construction of the strategic center of gravity) falls almost entirely within the civilian leadership's role (e.g., President Roosevelt during World War II). The U.S. military plays a largely bureaucratic role in constructing the traditional operational center of gravity through its institutional rather than operational components (that is, through U.S. Army Training and Doctrine Command rather than through, for example, the 3rd Infantry Division). In special warfare, the military, or whatever instrument the United States directs to implement policy, must often reintegrate into operational art what was native to its birth in the era of Napoleon by harnessing such forces as nationalism, sectarianism, or other mechanisms. In some cases, this will involve assisting in the construction of the strategic (moral) center of gravity necessary to mobilize a people.

Although the population may need to be mobilized to support a campaign effort, this, in itself, does not make it an operational center of gravity but, rather, a critical requirement (discussed later in this chapter). To become an operational center of gravity, the population must be sufficiently organized to be capable of collective action. Examples might include self-organization into protest movements, such as the anti-apartheid movement in South Africa, or action through other social or economic constructs, such as unions or tribes.

The operational center of gravity should always be understood as the principal means for seeking the desired end state, but its loss does not imply that the conflict ends. The continued existence of the strategic center of gravity implies that either the operational center of gravity will be reconstituted or a new one will be found. This is the dynamic that leads to the "mowing-the-grass" phenomenon sometimes observed in counterinsurgency: Where a new center of gravity is found, the nature of the conflict will likely change fundamentally (as in a shift from insurgency to terrorism).

A strategic center of gravity will rarely be an individual or even a set of individuals, unless the group lacks deep institutionalization or ideological roots. Sendero Luminoso (Shining Path) in Peru is an example of an insurgency with an ideology that was so personality-dependent that founder Abimael Guzmán was arguably its strategic center of gravity, and his loss sent the movement into a long-term decline. The destruction of the enemy's strategic center of gravity does not necessarily achieve a broader set of U.S. policy objectives beyond the discrete conflict. A fallen gun may be picked up by another hand. Following the FMLN's integration into El Salvador's national politics, there was a dramatic increase in crime, giving that nation the second highest murder rate in the world. Other insurgent groups have metastasized, transforming into criminal organizations. The dark network the United States helped build to support the counter-Soviet Afghan jihad became part of the infrastructure for global Islamist terrorism.

A center of gravity should not be treated as simply whatever is important in the campaign. It should also not be a proxy for a targeting matrix. Confusing centers of gravity with other elements of operational art distorts subsequent analysis.

Critical Capability
Critical capabilities are the primary abilities of a center of gravity used to defeat the enemy's means and will to fight.

In conventional operations, critical capabilities are principally lethal. In special warfare, nonlethal capabilities are likely to constitute critical capabilities, in addition to lethal ones. The conduct of information operations has been critical for al Qaeda and many other insurgent movements in degrading the legitimacy of targeted regimes and imposing additional costs on states' efforts to control the population and destroy insurgencies.

Critical Requirement
Critical requirements are the essential conditions, resources, and means for a critical capability to be fully operative.

In conventional operations, critical requirements are principally material. The brevity of modern U.S. conventional conflicts has rein-

forced this trend by reducing the requirement for broad domestic popular support, since major combat operations can be concluded even
before broad opposition can effect change through the electoral process. The protracted nature of special warfare makes broad domestic
support desirable, but its small footprint and modest costs can make
domestic indifference sufficient. For example, there has been little
debate surrounding U.S. efforts in the Philippines and only a small
amount regarding U.S. involvement in Colombia.

Within the targeted country, the population may possess critical
requirements that belligerents on both sides seek to access. Examples
include information, recruits, and material support.

Critical Vulnerability

A critical vulnerability is a decisive point to attack an enemy center of
gravity or critical requirement where the force may exploit an enemy
weakness.

In general, such critical vulnerabilities are rare among capable
adversaries. Candidates are either not critical (e.g., they are easily reconstituted or replaced) or not vulnerable (e.g., they are difficult to identify for targeting or embedded in cultural norms). That said, in special
warfare, vulnerabilities that can be exploited by information operations
can frequently be found in the gaps between the adversary's strategic
narrative and its tactical activities (e.g., abuse of the population). When
it comes to adversaries with low levels of institutionalization, whether
state or nonstate, targeting leadership can at times significantly disrupt
the belligerent's operations.

Decisive Point

A decisive point is a geographic place, specific key event, critical factor,
or function that, when acted upon, allows commanders to gain a
marked advantage over an adversary or contribute materially to achieving success.[23] Decisive points help commanders select clear, conclusive,
and attainable objectives that directly contribute to achieving desired
end states. Geographic decisive points can include port facilities, dis-

---

[23] U.S. Joint Chiefs of Staff, 2011a.

tribution networks and nodes, and bases of operation. Specific events and elements of an enemy force may also be decisive points. Examples of such events could include committing an enemy operational reserve and reopening a major oil refinery.

In special warfare, decisive points may still be geographic, but they may also be key events or critical factors. However, the details are likely different from those in a conventional campaign. Decisive points may be found in the local social order in the clans, tribes, castes, or classes that organize society and provide a recruiting pool for guerrillas and their auxiliaries. The adversary's computer network might be a decisive point if its ability to communicate, collect, process, store, and retrieve data is critical to its operations. Loss of third-party support or the internal consequences of profound governmental corruption could become decisive points in a special warfare campaign insofar as they limit the enemy's war-making capabilities and the commander is prepared to exploit these limitations.

More broadly, decisive points in special warfare are frequently hard to come by. Although particular special warfare operations or even campaigns are generally able to achieve their results relatively quickly (as was the case in the unconventional warfare campaign against the Taliban in 2001), special warfare typically resembles a marathon more than a sprint. Decade-long campaigns in El Salvador and Afghanistan are representative examples. That said, analysis of critical requirements and vulnerabilities can help identify potential decisive points; it may simply take longer to achieve the decisive effect.

Line of Operation

A line of operation defines the directional orientation of a force in time and space in relation to the enemy and links the force with its base of operations and objectives. Lines of operation connect a series of decisive points that lead to control of a geographic or force-oriented objective. Operations designed using lines of operation generally consist of a series of actions executed according to a well-defined sequence. A force operates on interior lines when its operations diverge from a central point or converge on the enemy. Operating on interior lines is frequently thought to confer the advantage of allowing the rapid concentration of forces at a decisive point. Exterior lines are thought to confer the advantage of enabling the envelopment of the enemy force. Combined-arms maneuver is often designed using lines of operation. These lines tie offensive and defensive tasks to the geographic and positional references in the area of operations.

In a special warfare campaign, a line of operation might concentrate on population centers, locations of symbolic significance, or more enemy-centric targets, such as lines of communication or basing (e.g., sanctuaries in adjacent states). In special warfare, the concepts of interior and exterior lines do not appear to contribute much insight above the tactical level, beyond what can already be achieved by identifying lines of communication.

Line of Effort

A line of effort links multiple tasks using the logic of purpose rather than geographical reference to focus efforts toward establishing operational and strategic conditions. Lines of effort are essential to long-term planning when positional references to an enemy or adversary have little relevance. In operations involving many nonmilitary factors, lines of effort may be the only way to link tasks to the end state. Lines of effort are often essential to helping commanders visualize how military capabilities can support the other instruments of national power.

Special warfare lines of effort are shaped by the unique character of special warfare. Typically, they should be derived from an analysis of centers of gravity and critical factors, and the commander's identification of decisive points. In FID operations, in particular, there appears to be some danger that lines of effort could standardized to reflect doctrinal "logical lines of operation": civil security, host-nation security forces, essential services, governance, and economic development.[24] This approach oversimplifies insurgency and counterinsurgency as a context-independent portable technology rather than an intensely conditional social phenomenon. One SOF graduate of the School of

---

[24] This follows the model outlined in FM 3-24, which recognizes that FID is distinct and unique from counterinsurgency (Headquarters, U.S. Department of the Army, and Headquarters, U.S. Marine Corps, 2014).

Advanced Military Studies who participated in the development
of an operations order for an operational-level headquarters in Afghanistan observed, "We copy lines of effort from the [counterinsurgency]
manual onto a PowerPoint slide, then argue for hours about whether
[information operations] should be a separate line of effort or a theme
running through all of them."[25]

The employment of special warfare capabilities can achieve syner-
gies through well-constructed lines of effort. As a FID example, host-
nation security forces can be deployed to deny the enemy freedom of
movement from safe havens, preventing fighters from massing on ethnically or geographically isolated communities. The isolated communities can then be protected by national police or local security forces,
depending on the capacity, capabilities, and locally perceived legitimacy of these forces. If the population has been alienated from the government, military information support or civil affairs operations might
be employed to create access for host-nation forces within the targeted
communities (e.g., through general interest in economic development
or by empowering a friendly local faction). The local security presence
can then develop networks of informants, enabling the employment of
precision-strike capabilities to interdict other clandestine enemy lines
of communication and safe havens. Collectively, this creates a security envelope in which state and friendly non-state actors can provide
valued services to the community. Military information support and
civil affairs activities might then focus on facilitating the organization of communities within secure areas for political activity, creating
a sense of stake in the current political regime. Ultimately, all of this
should increase state legitimacy, mobilizing communities to actively
support the state and contribute more to providing for their own security and well-being.

Insurgencies typically occur in places with weak levels of institutionalization, which permits abuse of the population at multiple levels
of government—from the police to courts and ministries. The application of special warfare methods might result in a modest U.S. force

---

[25] Interview by the research team, August 22, 2013.

presence in an advisory role at the local and national levels.[26] This U.S. presence would help manage a problem known as the principal-agent dilemma—when a "principal" employs an "agent" to act on its behalf at three levels:[27] (1) between the host-nation government and its forces and agencies in the field, (2) between the population and the national government, and (3) between the national government and the United States.

U.S. advisers in the field, such as special forces operational detachment alphas or civil-military operations center personnel, can identify conduct inconsistent with host-nation policy (e.g., corruption) and communicate the need for corrective action (e.g., replacement of host-nation military commanders or governors) to the host-nation's central government. Advisers embedded at the ministerial level can help develop the mechanisms for corrective action and facilitate their implementation. At the ministerial level, they can also observe whether or not the national government is actually demonstrating a commitment to the needs of the population and leverage U.S. interagency influence via diplomacy, foreign aid, information operations, or other mechanisms to pressure the national government to conform its behavior to the needs of the population. The collective insight of advisers at the tactical, national, the interagency level and consultation with a broad range of stakeholders can help the United States understand whether the host nation's actions are aligned with U.S. interests and what sources of influence the United States has that could credibly bring the host-nation government's behavior into alignment with U.S.

---

[26] A challenge at the national level is that the success of security ministries (e.g., defense, police, intelligence) often depends on the capacity of other ministries to promote economic development, justice, infrastructure, and other essential services. These capabilities are normally outside the expertise of military advisers, highlighting the fact that successful special warfare often requires an interagency effort.

[27] A principal-agent dilemma occurs when a principal employs an agent to conduct activities on the principal's behalf but there are limits to the principal's expertise or capacity and the agent's interests are not aligned with the principal's. As an example, you (the principal) might pay a mechanic (the agent) to fix your car. When the bill comes with many more repairs than you expected, you experience uncertainty about whether the additional repairs were needed or whether the mechanic is extracting additional profit by misrepresenting what repairs were needed, taking advantage of his specialized knowledge.

interests (e.g., threat of bank audit, support to other political parties with compatible interests). If change cannot be effected in the short term, the chief of mission or military commander might evaluate how to reduce U.S. commitments to the minimal level necessary to prevent the violation of core U.S. interests while employing longer-term efforts (e.g., economic development, civil society development, elections) to bring the host-nation government's interests into closer alignment with U.S. interests before reinvigorating U.S. military efforts. Lines of operation in this concept might be characterized as security, services, institutional, lethal, and nonlethal shaping.

In conventional operations, information operations are typically employed in support of maneuver operations, such as via leaflets dropped on Iraqi soldiers prior to ground operations in Operation Desert Storm. In special warfare, information operations may be supported by maneuver. Prime Minister Nouri Maliki's order for Iraqi brigades to conduct clearing operations in Basra was problematic from a strictly military perspective, but, at a political level, it served to deliver a potent message that the Iraqi government would be as intolerant of Shi'a militias that threaten the regime as it would of Sunni ones. Counterintuitively, in this concept, properly scoped maneuver would be a vital part of the nonlethal shaping line of effort.

Operational Reach
Operational reach is the distance and duration across which a joint force can successfully employ military capabilities. It reflects the ability to achieve success through a well-conceived operational approach. Operational reach is a tether; it is a function of intelligence, protection, sustainment, endurance, and relative combat power. The limit of a unit's operational reach is its culminating point (discussed later in this chapter). It equalizes the natural tensions between endurance, momentum, and protection. Operational reach is an operational art element that may require some adjustment for useful application in the special warfare context.

With respect to partners assisted via special warfare, instead of the "distance and duration across which military capabilities can be successfully employed," operational reach might be usefully reconceived in terms of the fighting season, the amount of time a guerrilla unit is capable of holding ground temporarily, or a given place. Subelements of operational reach, such as "endurance," might be understood in terms of the guerrillas' ability to operate for the duration of the fighting season. "Momentum" might be operationalized in terms of territory liberated or something similar. "Protection" might include considerations of available sanctuaries and liberated zones, as well as units located within mutually supporting distances of each other.

U.S. forces conducting special warfare may find their operational reach determined by the limits of their partners, including whether a partner's operational effectiveness is conditional on social or geographic terrain. For example, the Civilian Irregular Defense Group in Vietnam was effective when defending its own territory but ineffective in offensive operations.

Direct Approach
A direct approach involves applying combat power directly against an enemy's center of gravity.

The direct approach is certainly a significant feature of special warfare, in both FID and unconventional warfare, but the focus is on achieving effects through a partner's force.[28] A major distinction between special warfare and conventional conflict is that insurgents can, in many cases, control the rate at which their forces are destroyed, assuming they have secured a sanctuary (e.g., Taliban in Pakistan) or can maintain their operational security "among the people" (i.e., no one gives them up to the counterinsurgents). Under these conditions, insurgents can control their own rate of attrition by determining when to attack—differentiating themselves from the rest of the population

---

[28] The terms *direct* and *indirect* have different meanings in the conventional and special operations communities. The special operations community refers to the direct approach as U.S. unilateral efforts to achieve U.S. objectives, while it refers to the indirect approach as efforts to set conditions for others to achieve those objectives (e.g., SFA). To help integrate the two traditions, we use definitions from the conventional operational art literature (see, for example, those from the work of B. H. Liddell Hart, the military historian and theorist). We then explain how each concept applies in the context of special warfare. We feel the term *special warfare* largely coincides with the *indirect approach*.

and exposing themselves to counterattack—and when to acquiesce. In a special warfare campaign, U.S. forces may still play an important role in the direct approach through the provision of enablers (e.g., intelligence, fire support) or through supporting efforts (e.g., lethal counterterrorism activities, sabotage).

Indirect Approach

An indirect approach involves applying capabilities against critical requirements or vulnerabilities in ways that circumvent enemy strengths.

In special warfare, the United States seeks to apply all elements of U.S. and local partner power to affect and influence the enemy, not just "combat" power. The United States may also restrict the scale of its direct intervention to achieve broader operational or strategic objectives, such as preserving the local partner's legitimacy in the eyes of the population.

Tempo

Tempo is the relative speed and rhythm of military operations over time with respect to the enemy. It reflects the rate of military action. Controlling tempo helps commanders keep the initiative during combat operations or rapidly establish a sense of normalcy during humanitarian crises. In operations dominated by combined-arms maneuver, commanders normally seek to maintain a higher tempo than the enemy does; a rapid tempo can overwhelm an enemy's ability to counter friendly actions. It is the key to achieving a temporal advantage during combined-arms maneuver. During operations dominated by wide-area security, commanders act quickly to control events and deny the enemy positions of advantage. By acting faster than the situation deteriorates, commanders can change the dynamics of a crisis and restore stability.

Counterintuitively, in special warfare, actors may seek to maintain the initiative at the strategic level by moderating their operational tempo at the operational level. Rather than seeking to overwhelm the adversary's ability to cope by presenting it with the maximum number of challenges possible at a given moment, the supported local partner may instead seek to wear out the regime's external supporters and develop or preserve its own force long enough for the conditions for victory to present themselves.

Phasing and Transitions

A phase is a planning and execution tool used to divide an operation in duration or by activity. A change in phase usually involves a change of mission, task organization, or rules of engagement. Phasing helps in planning and controlling, and phase changes may be indicated by time, distance, terrain, or an event. The ability of Army forces to extend operations in time and space, coupled with a desire to dictate tempo, often presents commanders with more objectives and decisive points than the force can engage simultaneously. This may require commanders and staffs to consider sequencing operations. Transitions mark a change of focus between phases or between the ongoing operation and the execution of a branch or sequel. Shifting priorities among core competencies or among offensive, defensive, stability, and defense support of civil authorities tasks also involves a transition. Transitions require planning and preparation well before their execution to maintain the momentum and tempo of operations and to ensure that the conditions are right, including the host-nation's capabilities, for the transition to take place. The force is vulnerable during transitions, and commanders must establish clear conditions for their execution.

Dubik, in his treatment of operational art in counterinsurgency, essentially replaces decisive points with transitions of responsibility from the United States to the host nation.[29] The "notional operation plan phases" in JP 5-0, *Joint Operation Planning*, does little to illuminate the phases of special warfare.[30] FM 3-05.2, *Foreign Internal Defense*, offers another set of phases in a notional interagency plan: operational assessment, train and equip, direct support, indirect support, transition, and redeployment.[31] The special forces community has

---

[29] James M. Dubik, "Operational Art in Counterinsurgency: A View from the Inside," *Report 5: Best Practices in Counterinsurgency*, Washington, D.C.: Institute for the Study of War, May 2012.

[30] U.S. Joint Chiefs of Staff, 2011a.

[31] Headquarters, U.S. Department of the Army, 2011b.

long used a seven-phase model of unconventional warfare to represent engagement with and support to an insurgency.[32] The seven phases are as follows: preparation, initial contact, infiltration, organization, buildup, employment, and transition. This framework appears to be based on the Maoist protracted war model and is focused on the development and employment of guerrillas. It includes little focus on the underground and public elements of an insurgency (e.g., Sinn Fein in Ireland). Public elements of an insurgency may not always have visible links to the insurgency but nonetheless play an important role in the insurgents' strategy and typically enjoy clandestine coordination. That said, the model proved useful in abbreviated form for U.S. actions in Afghanistan in 2001 with the Northern Alliance and Iraq in 2003 with the *peshmerga*.

A common feature of all these models is a lack of focus on the political elements of an insurgency. The FID concepts of mobilization of the population and political neutralization of the insurgents are potentially powerful, but they require elaboration and the addition of political "integration" (see, for example, the cases of the FMLN and the Provisional Irish Republican Army, which were ultimately integrated into the political process). These concepts lie near the political heart of special warfare.

Culmination

Culmination is the point in time and space at which a force no longer possesses the capability to continue its current form of operations. Culmination represents a crucial shift in relative combat power. It is relevant to both attackers and defenders at each level of war. During offensive tasks, the culminating point occurs when the force cannot continue the attack and must assume a defensive posture or execute an operational pause. During defensive tasks, it occurs when the force can no longer defend itself and must withdraw or risk destruction. The culminating point is more difficult to identify when Army forces undertake stability tasks. Two conditions can result in culmination: units being too dispersed to achieve wide-area security and units lacking the

---

[32] Headquarters, U.S. Department of the Army, 2011a.

required resources to achieve the end state. While conducting defense support of civil authorities tasks, culmination may occur if forces must respond to more catastrophic events than they can manage simultaneously. That situation results in culmination due to exhaustion.

In special warfare it is clearly important for the United States to monitor and plan for the partner force's culminating point. But similar culminating points may exist on the path toward institutional reform. Political leaders usually speak of political capital as an exhaustible commodity. A partner force's strategic leadership, even if interested in reform, may be partly or entirely dependent on support from a military element with entrenched interests in the status quo. Stringent efforts to fully professionalize the behavior of a partner force could have perverse effects. Abstaining from extracting rents from the population or opting to preserve the equities of a movement's base by preserving leadership roles for coethnics might fatally undermine the state or movement's leadership. The political economy that sustains power is unique to each conflict, rendering efforts to make specific special warfare prescriptions that are portable across conflicts problematic at best. Therefore, adequately understanding the situation or the operational environment must involve considering the political and economic factors that may be difficult for SOF to influence. It is critical to identify all variables that may influence mission success—especially those that are difficult to leverage with special warfare. Avoid the temptation to assume that other agencies or actors will resolve these problems without adequate collaboration.

The United States may have its own culminating point in a special warfare campaign. These culminating points may be induced by resource or policy constraints typical of many special warfare campaigns, or by the exhaustion of domestic political support for a long-duration commitment.

Basing

A base is a locality from which operations are projected or supported. Bases or base camps may have a specific purpose (such as serving as an intermediate staging base, a logistics base, or a base camp), or they may be multifunctional.

In the unconventional warfare context, the menu of basing options might include considerations of sanctuaries in neighbor states, safe houses, liberated zones within the contested state, and perhaps contingency locations.

Risk

Risk is the probability and consequence of potential harm to the nation, the mission, or the force. Risk, uncertainty, and chance are inherent in all military operations. When commanders accept risk, they create opportunities to seize, retain, and exploit the initiative and achieve decisive results by focusing resources to accomplish priority objectives. Commanders rarely, if ever, have enough resources to cover every contingency. Therefore, they may accept risk in some areas to ensure success in others. The willingness to accept risk is often the key to exposing weaknesses that the enemy considers beyond friendly reach. Understanding risk requires assessments coupled with boldness and imagination.

Risk may be another operational art element that functions differently in special warfare than in conventional operations. As described in Army Doctrine Reference Publication 3-0, *Unified Land Operations*, risk is battlefield-oriented, and commanders treat it in concert with uncertainty, friction, and chance.[33] While this type of risk certainly applies in special warfare, commanders are likely to encounter a different, higher-order version of risk even before deploying. Unconventional warfare operations, almost by definition, take place beyond the operational reach of other U.S. forces. The President and Secretary of Defense, along with the GCC commander, must be confident that the unconventional warfare campaign in question can be accomplished successfully at acceptable levels of risk. The historical record indicates that senior U.S. leadership is often reluctant to commit forces under such circumstances.[34] When working with partner forces, the possi-

---

[33] Headquarters, U.S. Department of the Army, *Unified Land Operations*, Army Doctrine Reference Publication 3-0, Washington, D.C., May 2012b.

[34] For example, General Norman Schwarzkopf was reluctant to deploy special forces for special reconnaissance in Operation Desert Shield. Earlier in the 1980s, Congress imposed

bility of "green on blue" or insider threats may require trade-offs that entail the acceptance of risk.

The actor supported by a U.S. special warfare campaign will also have risk considerations, and these will be important for the U.S. commander and planners to understand and include in their calculations. While each actor's risk calculation will be *sui generis*, it is important to understand that these calculations will drive their actions.

These elements of operational art may be combined as depicted in Figure 3.3 to show the relationship between opposing forces at the operational level of war. Chapter Four considers how to apply these elements to special warfare.

Special Warfare Operational Art

> The first, the supreme, the most far-reaching act of judgment that the statesman and commander have to make is to establish . . . the kind of war on which they are embarking.
>
> —Clausewitz, *On War*[35]

> Mobilizing [popular] support was a political rather than a military task, and the primacy of political over military concerns became the hallmark of Mao's theorizing about warfare. In this respect he diverged markedly from traditional Western military thought, with its fairy rigid distinctions between war and peace, and between political and military affairs.
>
> —Shy and Collier, *Makers of Modern Strategy*[36]

The core observation that the heart of operational art begins with identifying the conflicting policy aims of the belligerents (conflicting ele-

---

force caps on advisory operations in Honduras and Nicaragua to limit the extent of U.S. involvement. Force protection considerations attended this decision.

[35] Clausewitz, 1984.

[36] John Shy and John W. Collier, "Revolutionary War," in Peter Paret, Gordon A. Craig, and Felix Gilbert, eds., *Makers of Modern Strategy from Machiavelli to the Nuclear Age*, Princeton, N.J.: Princeton University Press, 1986.

Figure 3.3
Joint Operational Art

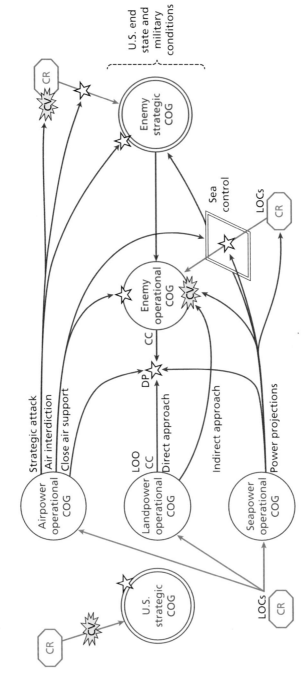

SOURCE: Michael Johnson, *Strange Gravity: Toward a Unified Theory of Joint Warfighting*, Ft. Leavenworth, Kan.: School of Advanced Military Studies, U.S. Army Command and General Staff College, 2001, p. 38, Figure 8.

NOTES: CC = critical capability. COG = center of gravity. CR = critical requirement. CV = critical vulnerability. DP = decisive point. LOC = line of communication. LOO = line of operation. Stars indicate decisive points. Green arrows correspond to lines of communication.

RAND RR779-3.3

ments of desired end states), the source of belligerents' will to prosecute the conflict (moral or strategic center of gravity), and the principal means by which the belligerents seek to exert their will (physical or operational center of gravity) is critical. This descent from the substance of the conflict, from the conflicting wills to what is fungible (to a degree)—the means employed—is important because it allows us to identify what is essential to the success of a campaign. The destruction or dislocation of the enemy's operational center of gravity (means) may, at times, be sufficient for the United States to impose the terms of peace. In other cases, the belligerents' particular means of exercising their will can be reconstituted (for example, by replenishing insurgent forces with fighters from a sanctuary) or other substitutes can be found (such as by employing irregular rather than conventional forces). The loss of will or the defeat of the enemy's strategic center of gravity, such as through a successful decapitation campaign against a centralized organization with little institutional depth or through an influence campaign alienating an enemy client state from its sponsor, removes the enemy's ability to replace its operational center of gravity. If the source of the conflict of wills can be removed (e.g., through a negotiated power-sharing agreement), then both the will and means to fight are rendered irrelevant—at least until a new "policy" objective is found for mobilized communities of violence (underscoring the importance of disarmament, demobilization, and reintegration programs).[37]

In practice, this analysis is iterative, with analysis of each component illuminating the others. It cannot be done in a vacuum, however; it requires a rich contextual understanding of a multiplicity of stakeholder perspectives. The joint political, military, economic, social, information, and infrastructure systems analysis approach is a useful construct for organizing thinking about the operational environment. The development of human intelligence networks and direct engagement with key stakeholders are critical tools used in special warfare to gain accurate situational understanding. Campaign planning cannot suc-

---

[37] For instance, underemployed revolutionaries enabled the rise of rampant criminality in El Salvador, and the end of the jihad against Russia in Afghanistan allowed the "Afghan Arabs" to refocus their resources on a global jihad.

ceed without this substantive understanding of the environment. The rich mosaic of actors involved in insurgency and counterinsurgency—whose objectives and means of pursuing them are often opaque to the United States until the process of engagement has begun—makes shaping operations and what the SOF community calls *preparation of the environment* critical.

This general phenomenon of planning and decisionmaking under uncertainty is not unique to special warfare. At the beginning of the Cold War, Washington had limited insight into the nature of the Soviet regime until the "long telegram" furnished essential insights, allowing Washington to outline a coherent policy for responding to the threat. What makes this issue uniquely important for special warfare practitioners is the greater dependence on partners from the strategic to the tactical level.[38] In U.S.-led (as opposed to partner-led) counterinsurgency efforts, the United States still has substantial autonomy to act and is often able to effect greater direct pressure on the partner's strategic leadership. For instance, Iraqi Prime Minister Maliki (a Shi'a) did not aggressively pursue the Sunni leaders whom the United States saw as critical to Iraq's interconfessional stability until after the withdrawal of U.S. troops. Special warfare requires working through and depending on partners to a greater extent than is the case when the United States has a substantial presence. The need to cooperate with partners provides the United States with what is often an ephemeral amount of leverage. However, this leads special warfare operational artists to design campaigns that are, in some ways, more sustainable.

In practice, U.S. special warfare campaigns are often conducted with partners with little institutional capacity and insufficient power relative to the adversary,[39] and this is why partners accept U.S. aid to begin with. The U.S. presence helps manage two levels of the inherent

---

[38] Watts et al., 2012.

[39] The range of institutional capacity exhibited by the Revolutionary United Front in Sierra Leone and Hezbollah in Lebanon demonstrate this is not simply an issue for state partners. Weinstein and Staniland have both written extensively on determinants of insurgent institutional characteristics. See Jeremy M. Weinstein, *Inside Rebellion: The Politics of Insurgent Violence*, New York: Cambridge University Press, 2007, and Paul Staniland, "Organizing Insurgency," *International Security*, Vol. 37, No. 1, Summer 2012.

principal-agent dilemma.[40] The first dilemma lies between the sometimes diverging objectives of the United States and the local partner (e.g., between the government or insurgent shadow government). The second dilemma lies in the divergence of interests between the partner force's political leadership and the force itself. Resolving the problem of combat power (or any other element of national power) may accomplish little if units in the field pursue their own narrow interests or if the interests of the partner diverge too sharply from those of the United States. *This makes the practice of sustained engagement to achieve influence a crucial contribution of special warfare.*

This logic leads us to the conclusion that special warfare operational art helps address three kinds of challenges in the effort to connect tactics to strategy:

- situational understanding
- influence
- capacity building.

Joint doctrine implies that *special warfare's unique contribution to operational art consists of the mobilization of partners' strategic and operational centers of gravity, and the neutralization or integration of the enemy's, in the human domain.* Conventional operational art enjoys the deployment of friendly operational centers of gravity and seeks to avoid risk to the friendly strategic center of gravity through rapid decisions on the battlefield. Special warfare generates friendly centers of gravity by mobilizing selected groups. Mobilization may occur in the narrow institutional sense of training and equipping a partner military or in the broader sense of mobilizing key segments of the population for action. Action might range from joining the military to organizing a protest movement or providing moral and material support.

---

[40] As noted earlier, the principal-agent dilemma occurs when a principal employs an agent to conduct activities on the principal's behalf but there are limits on the principal's expertise or capacity and the agent's interests are not perfectly aligned with the principal's.

CHAPTER FOUR

Organizing and Planning Constructs for Special Warfare

Planning special warfare campaigns involves more than the identification of elements of design. As one of our interviewees noted, the "campaign can't be just the plan."

In this chapter, we present a number of topics that are important for special warfare organization and planning and that, in some cases, are significantly different from normal military planning approaches. Examples include the need for special warfare campaigns to be nested in higher-level plans and policy guidance; the need to build consensus among disparate stakeholders, many of whom will not be military personnel or fall under the direction of any military headquarters; the importance of knowledge management and assessments; the importance of statutory authorities that authorize or preclude actions that special warfare planners might want to consider; and funding sources that can be used for one type of action but not another.

Understanding (and Influencing) Guidance, Objectives, and Constraints

The Chairman of the Joint Chiefs of Staff instructions for the Joint Strategic Planning System (JSPS) describe the process of formulating defense policy, military strategy, and campaign plans to provide advice and assessments to the Secretary of Defense and the President (see Figure 4.1).[1] The Adaptive Planning and Execution system (APEX) is used to integrate the activities of the joint planning and execution

Figure 4.1
JSPS Strategic Planning Battle Rhythm

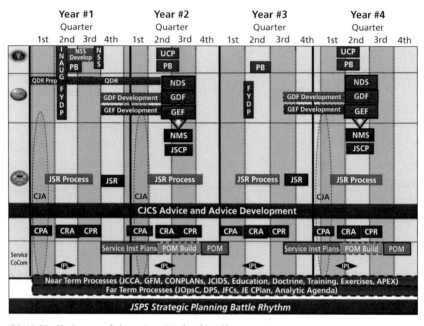

SOURCE: Chairman of the Joint Chiefs of Staff Instruction 3100.01B, 2013, p. A-8, Figure 3.

NOTES: CJA = comprehensive joint assessment. CJCS = Chairman of the Joint Chiefs of Staff. CONPLAN = concept plan. CPA = Chairman's program assessment. CPlan = campaign plan. CPR = Chairman's program recommendation. CRA = Chairman's risk assessment. DPS = defense planning scenario. FYDP = Future Years Defense Plan. GDF = guidance for the development of the force. GEF = guidance for the employment of the force. GFM = Global Force Management. IPL = integrated priority list. JCCA = Joint Combat Capability Assessment. JCIDS = Joint Capabilities Integration and Development System. JE = joint experimentation. JFC = joint functional concept. JOpsC = joint operations concepts. JSCP = joint strategic capabilities plan. JSR = joint strategy review. NDS = National Defense Strategy. NMS = National Military Strategy. NSS = National Security Strategy. PB = President's budget. POM = program objective memorandum. QDR =Quadrennial Defense Review. UCP = unified command plan.

RAND RR779-4.1

---

[1]   See Chairman of the Joint Chiefs of Staff Instruction 3100.01B, *Joint Strategic Planning System,* Washington, D.C., December 12, 2008, current as of September 5, 2013.

community engaged in contingency planning (see Figure 4.2). Within this system, SOF leaders can influence the development and employment of forces for special warfare in both deliberate and crisis action planning.

The Quadrennial Defense Review, National Defense Strategy, and National Military Strategy are high-level strategies that relate means to ends. The Guidance for the Employment of the Force and Joint Strategic Capabilities Plan provide strategic direction for imple-

Figure 4.2
Adaptive Planning Review and Approval Process

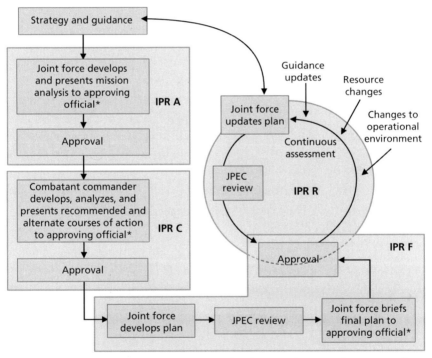

*Approving official is typically the Secretary of Defense or designated representative

SOURCE: U.S. Joint Chiefs of Staff, 2011a, p. I-4, Figure I-1.

NOTES: In-progress reviews (IPRs) are conducted by the Office of the Secretary of Defense or the Office of the Under Secretary of Defense for Policy. IPR A = strategic guidance. IPR C = concept development. IPR F = plan approval. IPR R = plan assessment. JPEC = joint planning and execution community.

RAND RR779-4.2

menting the defense and military strategies. These documents describe SOF roles for counterterrorism (i.e., direct action) and building partner capacity. However, the role of special warfare is barely touched on in these descriptions and never at the operational or strategic level. This important gap can be filled in the future as special warfare operational art understanding develops and strategic leaders better understand what it can deliver.

Below the national level, GCC commanders are tasked with developing strategies for their theaters of operations. However, there are typically few SOF planners on a GCC staff. SOF leaders and planners should help combatant commanders develop special warfare campaign options for their theaters that can be integral parts of the national approach.

Getting buy-in at national and GCC levels for special warfare approaches requires an explanation of what U.S. forces can and cannot achieve by working through partners. It is important for policymakers to set realistic objectives in accordance with special warfare capabilities if they want to take advantage of the small footprint that limits U.S. unilateral actions and to appreciate that special warfare approaches typically take time. To develop options for policymakers, and even to understand what constitutes "realistic" objectives, extensive activity may be required during the GCC's steady-state shaping phase, though the special warfare campaign may characterize these activities in different language. Such activities include PE. Regardless, special warfare planners may find that policymakers have a limited appetite for preventive activities that lack the immediacy of conventional crises (as in Iraq's invasion of Kuwait) and will need to be able to clearly link desired campaign activities to the outcomes that matter at a policy level.

Special operations are conducted as part of a broader campaign or JIIM effort, and thus should be fully nested within and consistent with the prescribed processes outlined in doctrine, policy directives, and other relevant guidance. This requires that special operations commanders and their staffs possess a deep understanding of the Joint Operation Planning Process and procedures employed at the supported command, as well as relevant planning processes of other governmental agencies, such as DoS and USAID regional and mission plans.[2] In particular, special operations estimates, proposals, and concepts of operation not only must be developed as part of the GCC's overarching theater strategy and theater campaign plan, but they must also be developed in a way (and with content) that is acceptable to other key stakeholders.

The locus of this planning activity will likely be the theater special operations command, the subordinate unified command that, by doctrine, is assigned responsibility for planning and conducting special operations in theater.[3] For plan development, approval, and execution to proceed seamlessly, SOF will need to undertake a sustained effort to communicate closely with GCC staff. Given that most staff officers and commanders are conventional personnel who rotate every few years, they may not be familiar with special operations, these operations' potential utility across the range of military operations, and the requirements for successful conduct of attendant core activities.

The resulting uneven relationship between theater special operations commands (TSOCs) and their parent (GCC) sometimes creates challenges to generating relevant, timely, and executable special warfare plans. Doctrinally, the TSOC commander holds three roles: joint force special operations component commander, special operations adviser to the combatant commander, and joint force commander.[4] Though the commander is identified as the special operations adviser, the TSOC is sometimes treated more strictly as a subordinate command that is directed to conduct independent planning based on concepts developed at the GCC level, rather than being directly integrated

---

[2] In addition to JP 5-0 and related doctrinal publications, an excellent resource is the *DoD Theater Campaign Planning: Planners' Handbook*, version 1.0, February 2012, published by the Office of the Deputy Assistant Secretary of Defense for Plans.

[3] There is discussion in the SOF community about the need for a headquarters capable of planning and executing special warfare campaigns that include SOF and conventional force elements. Should such a command or commands be developed, they could also fulfill this function. We return to this topic in Chapter Six.

[4] U.S. Joint Chiefs of Staff, *Joint Task Force Headquarters*, Joint Publication 3-33, Washington, D.C., July 30, 2012.

into the GCC initial planning process in the same manner as the command's organic staff.

Collaborative Planning for Unified Action

A critical element of the planning process will be the relationship between the United States and the partner force or government. In special warfare, U.S. efforts will have some of the characteristics of a "supporting command" in relation to the partner force. If the partner force is to be the main effort, then it will necessarily possess a sense of "ownership" over the campaign. In some special warfare cases, particularly those in which the partner force's commanders and planners have attended U.S. institutions (e.g., through the International Military Education and Training program), the partner's planning capacity may be very mature, and the partner may be seeking merely to leverage U.S. resources and capabilities to execute its campaign plan. Given that the United States will only rarely have interests and values that align perfectly with those of its partners, it will still need to develop a clear vision of how the campaign should unfold and, certainly, plan for how partners can best contribute.[5] In many cases, the partner force will not have sufficient training or doctrinal education to conduct campaign planning at the level of proficiency achieved by U.S. planners, driving its desire for U.S. intervention (and its associated resources). In those cases, U.S. planners will still lack the situational awareness of the partner force and will need to leverage it even as they enhance the partner's planning capabilities for the longer term through partnering and mentorship.

Today's complex and uncertain security environment requires campaign plans to be flexible and adapt as operations unfold. Special

---

[5]   For instance, in our El Salvador case study, although the El Salvador Armed Forces (ESAF) were professionally competent in campaign planning, they were not in a position to make judgments about political and judicial reform within their own country. U.S. pressure for those reforms would optimally be planned for by a U.S. special warfare task force in collaboration with and with guidance from the country team, National Security Council staff, and policymakers.

warfare efforts benefit from greater joint and interagency support when key partners are involved in the planning process. This implies a need to understand how to network and collaborate with relevant stakeholders in support of special warfare campaigns. This outreach will have to be tempered by operational security concerns, particularly in the case of compartmentalized clandestine activities, but even then, engagement with other elements of the U.S. government will be especially important.[6] Important findings are presented in this section, with a more complete treatment in Appendix B in the companion volume.

Most special warfare operations are conducted in coordination with conventional forces, other government agencies, or nongovernmental or international partners. In 2012 congressional testimony, Admiral William H. McRaven stressed the importance of building and sustaining relationships with key partners: "Through this network of relationships, SOF can provide a hedge against strategic surprise by identifying and working preemptively to address problems before they become conflicts."[7] Campaign planning, then, should include identifying and finding ways to incorporate inputs from diverse partners before operations or training programs commence. A shared understanding of the complex issues faced by a variety of actors and a means to communicate planning issues will help lay the groundwork for potential collaboration among diverse stakeholders. Having SOF liaisons in key nodes (in conventional force, interagency, international, and even nongovernmental entities) with the ability to connect and collaborate in support of campaign goals may help support SOF planning and coordination requirements.

---

[6] Interview by the research team, February 14, 2013. In addition to the cited research, the collaborative approach discussed later was informed by the experiences of a member of the RAND research team standing up a joint interagency task force in Iraq, managing USSOCOM's interagency task force, and designing operational-level SOF staff organizations in Afghanistan, as well as professional experience in collaborative planning in TSOC and embassy environments.

[7] ADM William H. McRaven, "Posture Statement of Admiral William H. McRaven, USN, Commander, United States Special Operations Command, Before the 112th Congress, Senate Armed Services Committee," March 6, 2012, p. 7.

Special warfare planning at the operational level requires the integration of diverse stakeholder equities to achieve unity of effort. To help address these challenges, several considerations for the successful management of multistakeholder initiatives are worth analysis in the early phases of planning:

- purpose, a specific issue, challenge, opportunity, or possibility that concerns all participants and provides the reason for convening
- people, a network of multiple state and nonstate actors to include representatives from government, business, nongovernmental organizations, academia, and civil society
- place, a space where participants meet in person (and, as needed, virtually) to collaborate
- process, a process of shared inquiry, learning, problem-solving, and (potentially) decisionmaking in new ways to address stakeholder concerns.[8]

Even U.S. government partners may not be pursuing common objectives, much less local or international partners. Who the appropriate partners are may not even be self-evident initially, in the absence of some measure of assessment. Where collaborative planning is called for, forums will need to be established. This may be particularly challenging given the variable security risk associated with different stakeholders. Given these challenges, careful consideration should be given to the process established for integrating partner objectives and lines of effort into a coherent campaign design.

In cases in which the core interests of the U.S. and partner diverge, a sustainable campaign may not feasible. Commanders will need to stress to their chains of command, and the theater commander to the policymakers directing the campaign (e.g., the Secretary of Defense), the nature of the risk associated with divergent U.S. and partner interests to drive a serious discussion about U.S. priorities. That does not

[8] Matthew Markopoulos, *Collaboration and Multi-Stakeholder Dialogue: A Review of the Literature*, version 1.1, Gland, Switzerland: International Union for Conservation of Nature and Natural Resources, Forest Conservation Programme, March 2012, p. 3.

mean that commanders and planners will not be tasked with developing just such a plan. But it will be necessary to have a common campaign plan with the partner in which objectives do nest. To address interests that are in conflict with the partner's, the United States will likely have to develop an overarching campaign plan that synchronizes its efforts in support of the partner with additional lines of effort.

Organizing for Unified Action

The practice of special warfare challenges the principle of unity of command in conventional operational art with its multinational, multiagency, multimilitary (or militant) organizations.[9] The confusion surrounding who should be in charge during special warfare operations and how those decisionmakers should be organized in practice is palpable in joint and Army doctrine.[10] When one considers the partitioning of sensitive activities, the challenge only becomes more pointed. One well-regarded planner of clandestine activities complained that there is "no institutionalized knowledge of who to reach out to—like herding cats. . . . . There's nothing comparable [to the interagency task force] for prevention. . . . Liaisons were the key problem."[11]

A key source of angst in the literature on special warfare organizational design is that its practice varies widely, as organization is highly dependent on the indigenous partner, U.S. stakeholders, and

---

[9] For a general discussion of the process of organizing a joint or joint special operations task force, see JP 3-33 (U.S. Joint Chiefs of Staff, 2012), JP 3-05 (U.S. Joint Chiefs of Staff, 2014), and Army Doctrine Reference Publication 3-05 (Headquarters, U.S. Department of the Army, 2012d).

[10] See Headquarters, U.S. Department of the Army, *Army Special Operations Forces Unconventional Warfare*, Field Manual 3-05.130, Washington, D.C., September 2008. One paragraph describes each phase of unconventional warfare, except for the organization phase, which takes four painstaking pages to describe. FID doctrine (JP 3-22, U.S. Joint Chiefs of Staff, 2010) weaves country teams with combatant commands, tactical units with agencies, and ambassadors with host-nation ministries and civil-military operations. Discerning some semblance of unified command of effort from complex circuitry diagrams and cloud conceptualizations is difficult at best.

[11] Interview by the research team, February 14, 2013.

any coalition or multinational stakeholders.[12] The operational art for designing a special warfare organization is more akin to improvisational jazz than a strictly orchestrated symphony. The organizations must begin as flexible, adaptable partnerships and grow into roles in which they are useful, rather than simply growing in ways that are easy, which can lead to large portions of a special warfare organization performing less-than-useful functions or to a neglect of difficult functions. During Operation Enduring Freedom–Philippines, Joint Task Force 510's initial (2001–2004) effort focused almost solely on ground operations on Basilan Island, until the command transitioned into Joint Special Operations Task Force–Philippines and gradually balanced its efforts to include combined maritime interdiction. The separatist insurgent Abu Sayyaf Group was most vulnerable in this domain, and, ultimately, maritime-based Philippine forces captured or killed most of the group's key leaders.[13]

Here, we put forward four critical considerations when developing a special warfare organization:

1. U.S. policy and resource constraints, including campaign objectives, desired signature, available forces, and other resource constraints
2. local partners, including their capabilities, legitimacy, and context
3. other partners, including U.S., coalition, and international partners contributing to the effort (knowingly or not)
4. the operating environment, including the threat and geography, among other constraints.

---

[12] We describe U.S. and multinational leadership here with the vague term *stakeholder* rather than the joint doctrinal term *command and control* because leading U.S. stakeholders may be agency chiefs, attachés, or development officers and not necessarily military commanders. For example, in special warfare, the military may simply provide a civil affairs team as a supporting effort to a DoS-led activity. The leadership variations become even more complicated when special warfare includes multinational stakeholders and their contributing organizations, agencies, and militaries.

[13] Molly Dunigan, Dick Hoffmann, Peter Chalk, Brian Nichiporuk, and Paul DeLuca, *Characterizing and Exploring the Implications of Maritime Irregular Warfare*, Santa Monica, Calif.: RAND Corporation, MG-1127-NAVY, 2012.

U.S. Policy and Resource Constraints

U.S. policy or resource constraints may dominate other considerations. One special warfare practitioner noted that U.S. SOF had "priced themselves out" of a recent special warfare operation by building a requirement for a joint special operations task force headquarters comparable in size to what has been used in Afghanistan or Iraq even though the proposed operation was much narrower in scope.[14] Planners should carefully analyze and distinguish between what is mission-essential and what is merely mission-enhancing. Policy and resource constraints that are too stringent for the campaign to be successfully executed should be explicitly identified and addressed by the commander.

Local Partners

The foremost consideration for a special warfare organization's design is the partner, its legitimacy, its capabilities, and the threats it faces. If the population views the United States poorly, a large special warfare organization can also damage a partner's legitimacy through association. However, the partner's capabilities and the threats it faces must also be considered together with legitimacy. If the security environment is too dangerous and unstable for the partner to survive, a larger special warfare organization that can provide more enablers may be necessary in the short term. Then, as (or if) the security situation improves, the special warfare organization can shrink to levels that better support the partner's image and legitimacy.

The partner's desires are important too, but they must be balanced against the commander's judgment of what is strategically and operationally best for U.S. objectives. The partner may want only U.S. air support and no advisers, while a special warfare commander may see that providing only U.S. air support will likely make the partner too reliant on the United State and hinder the partner's development toward the sustainable capabilities that its infrastructure can support. Moreover, a partner may want to seriously limit U.S. force levels to a point at which tactical mobility and medical evacuation are impossible at existing threat levels. U.S. commanders must work with the partner

---

[14] Interview by the research team, December 18, 2013.

to balance its desires with special warfare effectiveness. Because the local partner may be balancing a broad set of local considerations in which the commander has limited visibility, what is most effective for the special warfare campaign may not be immediately evident.

The partner's command relationships are also an important factor in designing a special warfare organization. If the partner centralizes political and military command and control, a U.S. commander may want to keep a larger headquarters colocated with the partner's headquarters and political offices or government ministries. If the partner decentralizes control with geographically arrayed task forces, a U.S. commander may more effectively assist with a similarly decentralized organization.

Liaison and adviser teams can be crucial players in special warfare because they provide the commander with key insights into the partner's political, military, and development components. They help coordinate efforts while also advising and assisting. Along with capable liaisons in key positions, special warfare command groups need to work to stay engaged with a partner's political, military, and development leaders by proactively seeking out and arranging relevant key leader engagements and continuously shaping the partner's efforts in constructive ways. Proactive key leader engagements and liaison officers with an initiative to help expand connectivity can build a special warfare organization into a more resilient network. Commanders should ensure that their adviser and liaison teams have a clear understanding of U.S. objectives and how those objectives may deviate from the partner's, avoiding unintentional incidents of teams becoming advocates for partners in ways that are detrimental to the campaign (i.e., "going native").

Other Partners

The next consideration for a special warfare organization is the array of U.S. and multinational organizations, agencies, and commanders involved in the effort to assist the partner's fight against the threats it faces. Special warfare commanders need to be responsive to the combatant commanders from whom they derive their authority, but they also need to maintain awareness and coordinate efforts with other, nonmilitary organizations. This coordination and connectivity may require liaison officers, or intelligence-operations centers, or civil-military operations centers.

The array of U.S. and multinational organizations in a special warfare campaign may require stovepiped structures to keep these activities separate from military operations. For example, aid organizations, such as Doctors Without Borders, typically do not want to be locally associated with military units for fear that adversaries might then consider their activities hostile and attack their personnel or restrict their movements. Similarly, intelligence agents or sources may not want to be associated locally with uniformed military units, as that would compromise their freedom of maneuver. To coordinate among these understandably stovepiped and locally separate functions in a special warfare campaign, intelligence-operations centers, civil-military operations centers, or other operation or coordination centers can facilitate connectivity and coordination at the national level while keeping local activities separate and discreet.[15]

Granted, decentralized execution is more efficient in combat operations, but in JIIM-supported special warfare operations, effective centralized coordination can be just as crucial. Centralizing functions while working with a partner whose political and security decision-making is also centralized allows a special warfare commander to keep the partner better informed, conduct more effective key leader engagements, and ensure that U.S. supporting efforts are predictable and in step with partner efforts. To satisfy these divergent needs, commanders may organize their forces as a mixed array.

Operating Environment

Other factors involved in organizing for special warfare include the forces available or allowed in country, adversary capabilities (the threat level), the permissiveness of the population, and local available resources, such as water, food, medical services, or transportation. If

---

[15] D. Hoffmann, *Civil-Military Coordination in Afghanistan*, Combined Forces Special Operations Component Command–Afghanistan Commander's Initiative Group Information Paper, November 5, 2010.

U.S. forces can subsist on local logistics, they can maintain a smaller footprint. Organizational adaptations used to adjust U.S. forces levels in country while also maintaining effectiveness include basing air support, quick-reaction forces, and medical evacuation units in a third country or afloat in international waters, and the use of national information, surveillance, and reconnaissance (ISR) capabilities or continental United States–based intelligence analysis via reachback communications. Reachback and regional basing can help a commander keep the in-country footprint small and discreet while maintaining adequate supporting forces to keep risk levels acceptable. Using reachback and regional basing also allows a commander to keep sophisticated ISR and sensitive intelligence data away from the partner's eyes and a safe distance from unstable environments. Special warfare requires U.S. forces to colocate with partners in most instances, and it helps foment a spirit of sharing and trust when those U.S.-only functions are located elsewhere so commanders can avoid the uncomfortable task of restricting a partner's access to buildings in its own sovereign territory.

Campaign Continuity and Knowledge Management

Campaign continuity and knowledge management are enduring challenges for long-duration campaigns. Military units execute tactical-level transfers of authority and reliefs in place, but this does not always happen effectively at the operational or strategic level when staff officers rotate out. Other times, lessons are captured but not always transferred into knowledge to benefit future efforts, and SOF commanders and staffs end up reinventing the campaign process. Strategic planners should be part of the transition process at the operational level, helping to connect incoming/outgoing commanders by sharing their understanding of the campaign's objectives, history, and assessments. Continuity would also benefit from commanders ensuring that lessons-learned personnel and unit historians incorporate operational- and strategic-level issues into their knowledge-capture process. Having a dedicated continuity process as an integral aspect of SOF operational-level planning would help create conditions for campaign continuity at the operational and strategic levels. Effective campaign continuity efforts require a dedicated knowledge management effort, including management of data and documents developed over the course of the campaign.

Assessments in Special Warfare

Assessments are critical to campaign success. Moltke famously observed that no plan survives first contact with the enemy. Assessments help commanders determine how to dynamically adapt their campaign plans to an evolving understanding of the enemy and operating environment.

Assessment is an immature field in joint operations in general and in special warfare in particular.[16] We divided types of assessments along temporal lines: prospective and retrospective. We refer to retrospective assessments of progress toward campaign or operational goals as *campaign assessments*, because this report is principally concerned with the operational level. We refer to prospective assessments of whether a given course of action is "feasible and acceptable" as *feasibility assessments*, in keeping with Army SOF doctrine.[17]

Doctrinal SOF tasks associated with assessments include area studies (conducted prior to deployment), area assessments (conducted throughout an operation), target audience analysis (conducted by military information support personnel), and civil information management (conducted by civil affairs personnel).

Feasibility Assessments

This capability is essential to find partners in areas of interest to the United States and to determine whether they have the potential to take actions that may be advantageous to the United States, as well as to

---

[16] Jan Osburg, Christopher Paul, Lisa Saum-Manning, Dan Madden, and Leslie Adrienne Payne, *Assessing Locally Focused Stability Operations*, Santa Monica, Calif.: RAND Corporation, RR-387-A, 2014; Connable, 2012.

[17] U.S. Joint Chiefs of Staff, 2011a; Headquarters, U.S. Department of the Army, 2012d.

recommend them as recipients of U.S. assistance (e.g., a special warfare campaign). The capacity for sound feasibility estimates is part of the frequently stated special warfare imperative to identify the right partners in the right places and to provide them with the right capabilities. The skills and knowledge required are formidable, however.

Often, potential resistance groups or power relations among elites are mysteries even within their own societies and therefore very difficult for outsiders to evaluate accurately. Feasibility estimates should be the work of personnel who, in addition to being steeped in the details of the subject, can anticipate potential second-order effects. For example, the decision to arm the mujahedeen against the Soviets in Afghanistan seemed wise until around 1995. The fighters had extracted a toll on the Soviet forces sent to Afghanistan, which was advantageous to Washington. However, the policy also sowed the seeds of a warlord-driven civil war and contributed to the circumstances that brought the Taliban to power. Arming the mujahedeen might still have been pursued, but with additional safeguards enacted to limit the scope of subsequent violence and political disorder.

Reflecting on a failed U.S.-backed coup attempt against Saddam Hussein, Mark Lowenthal, then–staff director of the House Intelligence Committee, said,

> All right, so we get rid of Saddam Hussein, good thing. But who do we get after him? . . . So this was a case where you had policy makers saying *do something*. This *do something* urge really expressed their frustration . . . [but the CIA] had no way to deal with Saddam Hussein. . . . It wasn't feasible. But it's very hard for an operator to say, "Mr. President, we can't do that." So you end up with an operation that probably shouldn't have been started in the first place.[18]

Feasibility estimating is a tough business, and special warfare commanders and planners should be cautioned that the U.S. track record has been poor when it comes to choosing suitable partners under much more favorable circumstances (e.g., when there is a large emigré popu-

---

[18] Tim Weiner, *Legacy of Ashes*, New York: Doubleday, 2007.

lation to choose from and U.S. officials can converse with candidates directly, as during the Cold War).

Campaign Assessments

Campaign assessment of any campaign is a bedeviling task that requires operators to identify measures that capture progress or setbacks and the information that would have to be captured to inform these measures. Assessment is always difficult, and must sometimes rely on questionable inputs in the absence of better information. Nevertheless, the question, "So, how are we doing?" is always lurking, and, especially in sensitive operations, is likely to come from many corners: the combatant commander, the Office of the Secretary of Defense, Congress, or the President. Assessment is therefore inescapable.

In general, there are two schools of assessment: quantitative (e.g., effects-based assessments, pattern and trend analysis) and qualitative (e.g., traditional unit reporting). JP 5-0 discusses campaign assessment in terms of metrics supporting measures of progress and effectiveness and is representative of quantitative assessment approaches.[19] Proponents of quantitative approaches argue that they are more objective and transparent than alternatives and may reveal trends and patterns that are not easily observed by commanders engaged in the day-to-day demands of combat. Quantitative approaches to assessment have come under criticism for a range of problems, however, ranging from methodological weakness to the quality of data.

Connable advocates a qualitative approach to assessments in which commanders at each echelon analyze their unit's progress against campaign objectives using methods similar to all-source intelligence analysis.[20] Observer bias (the "grading your own homework" problem) is addressed through the analysis conducted by each higher headquarters. These higher headquarters both synthesize the input of subordinates and assess the distinct campaign objects assigned to their echelons so that the final assessment is more than the aggregation of the small-unit assessments. Connable argues this approach better reflects the doctri-

---

[19] U.S. Joint Chiefs of Staff, 2011a.

[20] Connable, 2012.

nal foundations of campaign planning and the extraordinarily local-
ized conditions of irregular warfare, in particular. Regardless of which
approach is used, or whether some synthesis is employed, commanders
will still need to think carefully about how to relate the changing conditions of their environment to their campaign objectives.

The specific measures in use in any special warfare campaign
may differ depending on local conditions, circumstances, and campaign design. As an example, the following general types of questions,
if answered, may provide useful insights into the health of a resistance
movement, the quality of relations between the resistance and society, and the general state of the conflict in an unconventional warfare
context:

- The health of the resistance movement:
  - Is the guerrilla force growing in numbers?
  - Is the guerrilla force growing in capability?
  - Is the auxiliary force growing in numbers?
  - Is the auxiliary force growing in capability?
  - Is the underground growing in numbers?
  - Is the underground growing in capability?
  - Does the resistance enjoy popular support (e.g., "likes" on
    Facebook)?
  - Is the resistance spawning franchise operations at home or
    abroad?
  - Is the resistance attracting funding or other forms of assistance
    (indigenous, external)?
- Relations between the resistance and society:
  - Is the resistance penetrating society (e.g., are resistance-
    operated schools, clinics, courts being used)?
  - Does the resistance appear in social media? If so, is the view of
    the resistance generally positive?
  - Is the resistance able to collect taxes from the population? If so,
    from which communities or sectors?
  - Is the resistance tax base expanding? If so, into which com-
    munities?

- Does the resistance experience passive support from the populace (e.g., witnesses who "saw nothing")?
- Does the resistance have the active support of the population (e.g., are civilians misdirecting police searches, destroying evidence, or creating diversionary false alarms)?
- Does the population deliver tips to the police and security forces as to the identity and whereabouts of resistance members?
- General state of the conflict:
  - Which side enjoys greatest freedom of movement (by guerrilla command zone)?
  - Which side enjoys the best situational awareness (by guerrilla command zone)?
  - What is the ratio of weapons lost to weapons captured?
  - What is the trend in friendly force–initiated versus government-initiated incidents?
  - What is the trend in terms of standoff attacks (e.g., improvised explosive devices)?
  - What is the loss/exchange ratio with the enemy?
  - How many civil administrative units (e.g., villages, towns, counties, districts) are under resistance control?
  - How many civil administrative units (e.g., villages, towns, counties, districts) are under government control?
  - What levels of targets is the government attacking (e.g., guerrilla safe houses, bomb factories, media outlets)?
  - What type of targets is the resistance attacking (e.g., local civil targets, such as government buildings; military-police targets, such as checkpoints and garrisons; government officials)?

These lists of questions are not exhaustive, but they illustrate the types of information that could serve as the basis for special warfare assessments. These lists should not be used as a template for assessments. The commander will ultimately determine what measures to pursue based on the specifics of the case. If quantitative approaches are to be employed, it is important to hold the questions constant over time so that the answers can be used to establish trends relating to enduring campaign requirements. Beyond the core questions, questions addressing topical issues may be added or dropped. Every attempt should be made to answer the core questions at some regular interval: monthly, quarterly, or biannually, as appropriate for the measure's plausible rate of change. Questions should also be selected with consideration of the information required to answer them. Selecting questions solely because they are relatively easy to answer introduces a bias that favors "countability" over "significance." In some cases, despite the softness of the measure, it may be desirable to capture guerrilla chiefs' perceptions of progress, or those of SOF operators. As always, balance, richness, and nuance are important to good evaluations.

Subordinate commanders engaged in combat will have limited resources to dedicate to assessments, so it is important that these measures have a clear link to campaign objectives and the choices that the commander (or policymakers) will have to make.

Linking Assessments to Campaigns

Perhaps most importantly, assessments should be integrated with the process of campaign design. Measures of performance (MOPs) and measures of effectiveness (MOEs) should be directly tied to campaign lines of effort and objectives so as to reflect the commander's theory of how the campaign should progress, including the expected responses of the enemy, population, and government. Articulating the relationship between MOEs and MOPs and the campaign design may help commanders and staffs evaluate the campaign design for logical consistency (i.e., there is a logical chain of reasoning linking inputs, outputs, and outcomes).

At the operational level, MOPs relate to tasks that must be completed to properly execute a campaign plan. MOEs are oriented around end states and objectives and are used to determine whether or not the campaign plan's execution is leading to the desired results. If MOPs are advancing satisfactorily but MOEs are not, the commander should consider revising the campaign plan and revisiting assumptions—including whether selected MOEs collectively include necessary and sufficient criteria for achieving the desired end state. Critical assumptions underlying the campaign design should be explicitly identified and tested through the assessment process to assist in the "reframing" process of the Army Design Methodology.[21]

MOEs and MOPs should not be purely quantitative; rather, they should explicitly and transparently incorporate the qualitative insights of both commanders and staffs (e.g., through narratives rather than opaque color-coding exercises), as well as other sources (e.g., public opinion polling). Single-source assessments, in which all metrics are based on input from one observer, should be treated with the same caution as single-source intelligence reports. Commands will have to build processes, business rules, and means for collecting and analyzing data and reporting needed to support an effective assessment process. One possible place to collect these data is the Combined Information Data Network Exchange (CIDNE), a repository for tactical-level information.

As noted earlier, operations and feasibility assessments are still a nascent art requiring additional research and testing, and a detailed examination of these points was beyond the scope of this study.

Resources and Authorities for Special Warfare

Commanders and planners should recognize that a sound campaign plan is a necessary prerequisite for successful requests for resources and authorities. Without a clear campaign plan to support new requirements, the Joint Staff, the Office of the Secretary of Defense, and Congress are unlikely to perceive a compelling need to provide new resources and authorities. A well-constructed campaign plan will identify required authorities and required tasks. When the Secretary of Defense approves the plan, the execution order will provide the authority to execute those tasks.[22]

---

[21] For more on the Army Design Methodology, see Army Doctrine Reference Publication 5-0 (Headquarters, U.S. Department of the Army, 2012a).

[22] For example, Dave Maxwell has noted that the campaign plan in Operation Enduring Freedom–Philippines included a task to train host-nation police forces. Typically, the U.S. military is prohibited from training interior ministry personnel. Once the execution order was signed, the U.S. military (along with the Federal Bureau of Investigation and other

Understanding the enabling or constraining authorities that govern special warfare will help SOF commanders more effectively manage necessary relationships during the planning and execution of their operations. The past decade has seen a dramatic evolution of SOF capabilities, responsibilities, and authorities. U.S. Special Operations Command (USSOCOM) has attempted to maintain and enhance the authorities it has gained from this experience, though these authorities may continue to fluctuate and change. It is imperative for commands conducting special warfare to maintain a thorough understanding of current funding, oversight, and execution authorities, because, "without authorities, a team will not know its limits and could easily exceed them, or it might operate well below what is allowed and miss critical opportunities to interdict a problem."[23]

The overlapping patchwork of authorities that govern SOF activities often requires SOF commanders to "cobble together a collection of authorities, each with unique stakeholders and approval and notification processes," with "mismatched timelines and multiple points of potential management friction."[24] Given the potential increase in demand for SOF and special warfare capabilities in the future, it is imperative that SOF commanders, as well as conventional force commanders, pursue special warfare operational art with a working knowledge of these authorities and reporting requirements.

To ensure the availability of adequate resources, authorities, and permissions to execute a special warfare campaign, planners should understand the following authorities and processes, discussed in greater depth in Appendix C in the companion volume:

---

government agencies) was able to train the Philippine National Police. Interview with Dave Maxwell, Washington, D.C., April 12, 2013.

[23] Kevin Wells, "8 Years of Combat FID: A Retrospective on SF in Iraq," *Special Warfare*, Vol. 25, No. 1, January–March 2012.

[24] Michael Sheehan, Assistant Secretary of Defense for Special Operations and Low-Intensity Conflict, *Future Authorities That May Be Necessary for Special Operations Forces to Adequately Conduct Counterterrorism, Unconventional Warfare, and Irregular Warfare Missions: Report to Congress in Compliance with the Reporting Requirement Contained in Sub-Section (d) of Section 1203 of the National Defense Authorization Act for FY 2012 (P.L. 112-81)*, January 11, 2013, p. 8.

- APEX and existing execution orders[25]
- the Global Force Management and Request for Forces processes
- Planning, Programming, Budgeting, and Execution process—not to become a budgeting expert but to understand how deliberate planning (e.g., operation plans) can support combatant command and force provider program requests, setting the conditions for future operations
- chief of mission and combatant commander authorities
- the distinction between clandestine and covert operations.

There are several resourcing authorities with particular relevance to special warfare. Relevant general DoD funding authorities include the following:

- Global Train and Equip, commonly known as Section 1206, authorizes up to $350 million for the Secretary of Defense, as directed by the President with the concurrence of DoS, to build the capacity of a foreign country's national military forces to "conduct counterterrorist operations" or "participate in or support military and stability operations in which the United States Armed Forces are a participant."[26] This authority was established to address the need for "a response for emergent threats or opportunities in six months or less."[27] The program uses single-year funds but has been reauthorized every year since its introduction in 2005. Despite its popularity with the GCCs, Section 1206 programs are typically limited to three years, after which they are

---

[25] For more on APEX, see JP 5-0 (U.S. Joint Chiefs of Staff, 2011a).

[26] *Section 1206* refers to the program's place in the National Defense Authorization Act for Fiscal Year 2006 (see Public Law 109-163, National Defense Authorization Act for Fiscal Year 2006, January 6, 2006).

[27] U.S. Department of Defense, *Fiscal Year 2009 Budget Request Summary Justification*, Washington, D.C., February 4, 2008, p. 103. For further details on the history of DoD's increased involvement in SFA, see Nina M. Serafino, *Security Assistance Reform: "Section 1206" Background and Issues for Congress*, Washington, D.C.: Congressional Research Service, April 19, 2013.

"transitioned to more traditional security assistance authorities," such as those under Title 22 of the U.S. Code.[28]

- The Global Security Contingency Fund was established to "address rapidly changing, transnational, asymmetric threats, and emergent opportunities" in "countries designated by the Secretary of State, with the concurrence of the Secretary of Defense." Monies from the fund are available to either DoS or DoD. The assistance, including equipment, supplies, and training, is for security programs, as well as justice-sector and stabilization programs. The security programs entail enhancing "the capabilities of a country's national military forces, and other national security forces that conduct border and maritime security, internal defense, and counterterrorism operations, as well as the government agencies responsible for such forces." Justice-sector and stabilization programs include law enforcement and prisons, rule-of-law programs, and stabilization efforts in which the "conflict or instability in a country or region challenges the existing capability of civilian providers to deliver such assistance." The fund's applicability to the partner nation's interior security forces and justice sector distinguishes it from most other DoD funding authorities.[29]
- The Combatant Commander Initiative Fund allows the Chairman of the Joint Chiefs of Staff to provide funding to the "commander of a combatant command" or "an officer designated . . . for such purpose" outside the area of responsibility of a combatant command.[30] Among other activities, the statute allows, across the combatant commands, up to $5 million in funds for military education and training to be provided to military and related civilian personnel of foreign countries and up to $10 million for foreign countries participating in joint exercises. Funds may not be used for activities denied authorization by Congress. Theater

[28] Sheehan, 2013, p. 11.

[29] Nina M. Serafino, *Global Security Contingency Fund: Summary and Issue Overview*, Washington, D.C.: Congressional Research Service, April 4, 2014, pp. 1, 4.

[30] 10 U.S.C. 166a, Combatant Commander Initiative Fund.

SOF occasionally execute these activities when the GCC requests this funding.

- Section 1206 in the National Defense Authorization Act for FY 2012, "Support of Foreign Forces Participating in Operations to Disarm the Lord's Resistance Army (CLRA) Logistics Support," though DoD-managed, requires the concurrence of the Secretary of State for any logistics, supplies, or service support funding. Combat operations by U.S. personnel in connection with this provision are prohibited.[31]

- The Combating Terrorism Initiative Fund, Combat Mission Requirements Fund, Commander's Emergency Response Program, and the DoD Rewards Program are described in the U.S. Code.[32]

- Emergency Extraordinary Expense funds may be provided for an emergency or extraordinary expense that is unanticipated or classified in nature.[33] The Secretary of Defense must notify the House and Senate Committees on Armed Services and Appropriations when the funds expended are greater than $500,000 on certain timetables determined by the amount to be spent, unless the Secretary of Defense determines that compliance will compromise national security.[34]

- Confidential Military Purpose funds are "expended upon the approval of the Secretary of the cognizant Military Service and payment may be made on their certificate of necessity for confidential military purposes."[35] These operations and maintenance

---

[31] Public Law 112-81, National Defense Authorization Act for Fiscal Year 2012, December 31, 2011.

[32] 10 U.S.C. 166b, Combatant Commands: Funding for Combating Terrorism Readiness Initiatives; 10 U.S.C. 167, Unified Combatant Command for Special Operations Forces; 10 U.S.C. 127, Assistance in Combating Terrorism: Rewards.

[33] 10 U.S.C. 127.

[34] In which case the Secretary immediately notifies the committees that the obligation or expenditure is necessary and then provides relevant information to the committee chairs and ranking minority members.

[35] Pub. L. 112-10, 2011.

expenses entail the same limitations as for Emergency Extraordinary Expense funds.

Relevant SOF-specific funding authorities include the following:

- The Joint Combined Exchange Training (JCET) statute[36] allows funding for deploying to and training with a partner nation if the primary purpose of the training is "to train the special operations forces of the combatant command." JCET also covers "incremental expenses" incurred by the partner nation if it is a "friendly developing country," though it does not cover military construction or leave-behind equipment. The exchanges are short, typically 60–90 days, and are episodic in nature.[37] JCETs should not be confused for SFA authority; by statute they are designed to support U.S. SOF training, not FID or unconventional warfare campaigns.
- Section 1208 authorizes up to $50 million annually for SOF "to provide support to foreign forces, irregular forces, groups, or individuals engaged in supporting or facilitating *ongoing military operations by United States special operations forces to combat terrorism.*"[38] This DoD-funded authority therefore must have a counterterrorism focus and cannot be used for general SFA. Under Section 1208, units typically receive requested equipment, supplies, and related training through the USSOCOM acquisition process within 60 days.[39] Subsequent amendments since the authority was established in 2004 have added more detailed reporting requirements, as well as a requirement for relevant chief of mission concurrence.[40] This section does not authorize covert

---

[36] 10 U.S.C. 2011, Special Operations Forces: Training with Friendly Foreign Forces.

[37] Sheehan, 2013, p. 12.

[38] Public Law 108-375, National Defense Authorization Act for Fiscal Year 2005, October 28, 2004; emphasis added.

[39] Sheehan, 2013.

[40] Chief of mission concurrence was added in 2008. The additional reporting requirements entail providing congressional defense committees, before the exercise of the authority,

activities. As of this writing, Section 1208 authority was set to expire in FY 2015.

Effectively leveraging these resources will require planners to have a strong understanding of the DoD budget process, and military services' POM cycle.

---

with the following:

> A description of supported operations; a summary of operations; the type of recipients that received support, identified by authorized category (foreign forces, irregular forces, groups, or individuals); the total amount obligated in the previous fiscal year, including budget details; the total amount obligated in prior fiscal years; the intended duration of support; a description of support or training provided to the recipients of support; a value assessment of the operational support provided. (Public Law 111-84, National Defense Authorization Act for Fiscal Year 2010, October 28, 2009, Section 1202)

CHAPTER FIVE

Applications of Special Warfare Operational Art

Special warfare campaigns appear to have a comparative advantage in the joint repertoire in which U.S. interests drive policymakers to action, yet they seek to avoid committing conventional U.S. forces out of concern for efficacy, escalation risk, or cost when recourse to stand-off fires is unlikely to achieve U.S. goals (e.g., when the regime's core interests are at stake). For example, a threat could become significant if allowed to develop unaddressed, but it could also be positively affected by local actors and, given sufficient resources, support, and time, would be a candidate for a special warfare campaign. Under these conditions, special warfare may present the most effective solution.

Having identified the unique characteristics of operational art in special warfare (see Chapter Three), we apply this framework to two case studies to test whether the concepts of mobilization and neutralization illuminate their conduct using center-of-gravity analysis.[1] We find that they do.

We largely retain the language of Clausewitz and his doctrinal interpreters because it is broadly familiar to the practitioner community and used in combatant command plans. This leaves us with the following framework for analyzing these cases:

- belligerents' conflicting end states
- strategic center of gravity
- operational center of gravity

---

[1] The center-of-gravity analysis used here is based on the history of the conflict rather than the original operational plans.

- critical capabilities, requirements, and vulnerabilities
- decisive points
- lines of operation and effort.

This list is not intended to diminish the importance of other elements of operational art, such as operational reach, basing, tempo, phasing and transitions (treated as functional decisive points where relevant), culmination, and risk. Our analyses of the case studies are intended to be parsimonious rather than doctrinally comprehensive. These elements of operational art were selected because we determined that, without their proper identification, none of the other elements could be coherently assessed.

We selected the El Salvador and Afghanistan cases because they illustrate each of the five characteristics of special warfare campaigns: local partners providing the main effort, influence activities for mobilization and neutralization, small footprint, long duration, and leadership by other U.S. government agencies. In particular, the United States was faced with the challenge of working through problematic partners with preferences that diverged from those of the United States at either the institutional (ESAF in El Salvador) or policy level (Pakistan in Afghanistan), in some ways making them representative of the central challenge of special warfare.

After presenting the two case studies, we describe several notional campaigns in which special warfare might be employed to address strategic challenges of special relevance to policymakers. It is our hope that these scenarios will help provide a broadened base for the analysis of special warfare requirements, enhance thinking about the application of operational art in future experiments and exercises, and illuminate the applicability of special warfare to today's challenges.[2]

---

[2]   Observation by the research team, January 23, 2013. Some of our interviewees also felt that the current unconventional warfare model remains too tied to the Maoist model of rural insurgency.

Foreign Internal Defense: El Salvador, 1979–1992

Over the course of the civil war between the FMLN and El Salvador's government, 80,000 people were killed (out of a population of approximately 5 million), and a quarter of the population was displaced. The conflict began in 1979 with a military coup and the coalescence of leftist guerrillas to overthrow the new junta the following year. Having come to a military stalemate, the parties signed a final peace accord in 1992 that addressed socioeconomic inequalities and authoritarianism through land and political reforms and asserted civilian control of the military.[3] Military reforms included reductions in El Salvador's overall force size, a purge of human rights violators in its ranks, and the transfer of responsibility for internal security from the military to a new civilian police force. Since the accord was signed, El Salvador has continued to enjoy peace and economic growth. However, the limits to this progress were highlighted by the "300-percent increase in violent crime in the first nine months of 1993,"[4] and, today, El Salvador suffers from the world's second highest homicide rate.

Over the course of ten years, the United States provided El Salvador with $6 billion in assistance, as well as military trainers and advisers. Congress restricted the number of military advisers to 55, and these advisers were prohibited from participating in combat operations. In practice, they did not advise below the brigade level and, at that level, only several years into the effort. FMLN commander Joaquin Villallobos believed that "putting American advisers in the brigades was the most damaging thing that happened to [the FMLN] during the war. He believed that the advisers' influence on the [El Salvadoran military] made them more professional and less abusive, . . . [denying the FMLN] much of its earlier propaganda advantage and recruiting appear."[5] The FMLN also requested that the U.S. advisers remain with the brigades during demobilization.

---

[3] For example, in terms of political reform, the FMLN was allowed to compete in elections after certification of disarmament.

[4] Dobbins et al., 2013, p. 86.

[5] Quoted in D. Jones, 2006, p. 106; omissions and bracketed text in original.

The U.S. administration perceived that the core U.S. interest in the conflict was preventing the spread of communism, with a secondary interest in democratic reform and respect for human rights given force by congressional pressure. The end of the Cold War, fiscal assurances from the United States to both parties, and United Nations (UN) mediation were all critical to establishing the peace agreement, but it was U.S. FID support that preserved the regime long enough for the geopolitical situation to evolve, setting the conditions for a negotiated peace.

Conflict Narrative

El Salvador was, in many ways, not a promising prospect for a FID mission. When a coup occurred in 1979, the country was essentially a feudal society with a "kleptocratic and dictatorial" government and a "corrupt, barracks-bound" military.[6] The military was infamous for its abuse of the population and was associated with death squads. Ultimately 85 percent of human rights violations committed during the conflict were attributed to government forces.[7]

FMLN forces were able to prosecute an almost conventional war—what is called mobile warfare in the unconventional warfare literature—for the first several years of the insurgency. From 1980 to 1983, they operated in rural areas in units with several hundred members. At its peak in the early 1980s, the FMLN controlled perhaps as much as 33 percent of El Salvador,[8] and it fielded as many as 12,000 fighters.[9] The FMLN forces were more effective than the Salvadoran military and better liked by the population. In 1981, after the near success of what the FMLN had optimistically termed its "final offensive,"

---

[6]   Christopher Paul, Colin P. Clarke, and Beth Grill, *Victory Has a Thousand Fathers: Sources of Success in Counterinsurgency*, Santa Monica, Calif.: RAND Corporation, MG-964-OSD, 2010, p. 13.

[7]   Between 40,000 and 50,000 civilians are estimated to have been killed by state forces.

[8]   Dobbins et al., 2013.

[9]   Michael Childress, *The Effectiveness of U.S. Training Efforts in Internal Defense and Development: The Cases of El Salvador and Honduras*, Santa Monica, Calif.: RAND Corporation, MR-250-USDP, 1995.

the Reagan administration chose to restore military aid to the Salvadoran government (restricted following the coup), sending in several military adviser teams just days after the assault.

That same year, Brigadier General Frederick Woerner led a "military strategic advisory team" to El Salvador to assess the situation, help develop a national military strategy, and establish a U.S. military assistance program. His report advocated expanding the number of Salvadoran battalions by two-thirds, to 25, as well as increasing the force's professionalism, capability modernization, and aggressive use of small-unit patrols. General Woerner warned,

> Unabated terror from the right and continued tolerance of institutional violence could dangerously erode popular support to the point wherein the Armed Force would be viewed not as the protector of society, but as an army of occupation. Failure to address the problem will subject the legitimacy of the Government of El Salvador and the Armed Force to international questioning.[10]

The 1982 election of President José Napoleón Duarte created a sufficient perception of legitimacy to set the conditions for U.S. military aid to greatly increase with congressional support. Ultimately, the Salvadoran military force was expanded from 11,000 to 56,000 personnel.

Salvadoran units were sent to a regional U.S. training center in Honduras, and 500 officers were sent to the United States for training. The U.S. advisers embedded in the Salvadoran brigades appear to have received little training or guidance specific to El Salvador, apparently under the assumption that no operational guidance was required. Until 1984, the focus appears to have been on the rapid expansion of the force, at some cost to leadership quality in an already problematic military culture.

Nonetheless, combat effectiveness improved, and, by 1985, the FMLN was forced to revert to small-unit guerrilla warfare. U.S. train-

---

[10] Quoted in Robert D. Ramsey, *Advising Indigenous Forces: American Advisors in Korea, Vietnam, and El Salvador*, Global War on Terrorism Occasional Paper 18, Ft. Leavenworth, Kan.: Combat Studies Institute Press, 2006, p. 85.

ing of the Salvadoran "rapid-reaction" battalions was also critical to moving the military out of the "strategic defensive."[11] The Salvadoran military was reluctant to conduct small-unit counterinsurgency tactics advocated by U.S. advisers, preferring to operate in at least battalion-sized units and the liberal employment of air and artillery fire support. "Looking back, a former MILGROUP commander noted that early [Salvadoran military] operations of big sweeps and multi-battalion operations 'looked like a repeat of the American Way of War, namely, bigger, louder and more of the same.'"[12]

Even by 1987, the Salvadoran military appeared unable to conduct both offensive operations and civic action programs as part of an integrated counterinsurgency campaign, though at that point, capacity may have been a constraint. Some analysts argue that ESAF had become a "force that combined small unit operations, intelligence, civic action, psychological operations, protection of economic infrastructure, and winning the support of the population."[13] In areas taken back from guerrillas, the government made efforts to rebuild infrastructure through civil action programs. El Salvador also built another common counterinsurgency tool, local security forces, via the Civil Defense Program. The program, with the support of U.S. Ambassador Thomas Pickering, was developed and run by a U.S. special forces sergeant. Unfortunately, the program, like the rest of the military, was tainted by association with death squads.[14] Sympathetic observers in 1988 determined that the military's human rights abuses had been

---

[11] Angel Rabasa, Steven Boraz, Peter Chalk, Kim Cragin, Theodore W. Karasik, Jennifer D. P. Moroney, Kevin A. O'Brien, and John E. Peters, *Ungoverned Territories: Understanding and Reducing Terrorism Risk*, Santa Monica, Calif.: RAND Corporation, MG-561-AF, 2007.

[12] Ramsey, 2006, p. 95.

[13] Robert J. Molinari, *Carrots and Sticks: Questions for COCOMs Who Must Leverage National Power in Counter Insurgency Warfare*, thesis, Newport, R.I.: Naval War College, 2004, quoted in Tompkins and Crossett, 2012.

[14] Austin Long, Stephanie Pezard, Bryce Loidolt, and Todd C. Helmus, *Locals Rule: Historical Lessons for Creating Local Defense Forces for Afghanistan and Beyond*, Santa Monica, Calif.: RAND Corporation, MG-1232-CFSOCC-A, 2012.

somewhat reduced and that U.S. efforts had been successful in leading the military to accept civilian control.[15]

A stalemate lasted from 1987 to 1990. In 1989, frustrated with stalled talks, the FMLN attempted major urban assaults. The Salvadoran military was surprised, responded ineffectively, and continued to engage in human rights abuses. After several Jesuit priests were murdered, Congress cut military aid to the country by 40 percent. The United States was unsuccessful in improving the military's treatment of human rights until after the conflict concluded.[16] Neither was USAID able to effect the land or judicial reforms it advocated. Perhaps the fundamental challenge of FID with flawed partners was best summarized by Childress in his review of U.S. efforts in El Salvador:

> As the United States has attempted to train the skills applicable to internal defense and development, it has faced three fundamental hurdles. First, can the United States effect basic attitudinal and behavioral change in the individual soldier who receives the training? Second, assuming the individual soldier internalizes the lessons on "professionalism," can this individual-level metamorphosis be translated into a wide institutional transformation? Third, given the multitude of exogenous factors that affect democratic political development and structurally induced political repression, can the military play an instrumental role in effecting change on a societal level? Strong political, personal, historical, and financial reasons abound for these militaries to remain politically viable and independent. Consequently, it would appear that no amount of U.S. training could persuade them to do otherwise.[17]

The United States has sometimes found, to its regret, that good tactics do not add up to good strategy. In this case, modestly effec-

---

[15] Ramsey, 2006.

[16] Seth G. Jones, Olga Oliker, Peter Chalk, C. Christine Fair, Rollie Lal, and James Dobbins, *Securing Tyrants or Fostering Reform? U.S. Internal Security Assistance to Repressive and Transitioning Regimes*, Santa Monica, Calif.: RAND Corporation, MG-550-OSI, 2006.

[17] Childress, 1995.

tive tactics, when framed within a coherent strategy, were sufficient to secure core U.S. interests.

Application of Operational Art
Belligerents' Conflicting End States

The United States and El Salvador both opposed the communist FMLN. While the United States also sought democratic and human rights reform, this was ultimately of secondary consideration so long as El Salvador was seen through the lens of the Cold War. The FMLN sought power and a broad range of socioeconomic reforms, while Cuba and Nicaragua were believed to see it as an opportunity to continue spreading the communist revolution.

Strategic Centers of Gravity

The U.S. strategic center of gravity in this conflict was the U.S. alliance with El Salvador's government against communism in that country. The FMLN's strategic center of gravity was its alliance with Cuba and Nicaragua to perpetuate the spread of communism in El Salvador. Both alliances marked the boundaries of acceptable policy outcomes and shaped the means available for prosecuting the conflict, as discussed later in this chapter. An argument could be made that the U.S. strategic center of gravity shifted during the conflict, becoming more dependent on President Duarte's personal prestige as a reformer and anticommunist (rather than the legitimacy of El Salvador's government, per se), which held together the alliance of the U.S. administration, Congress, and El Salvador's military.[18] The FMLN's policies and cohesion did not appear to depend to a great extent on personality.

Operational Centers of Gravity

El Salvador's military (ESAF) was the principal means for the United States to combat the FMLN, and the U.S. advisory teams were the principal means of influencing ESAF. Arguably, the U.S. operational

---

[18] The fact that U.S. support to El Salvador predated the elections argues against President Duarte's role as a strategic center of gravity. However, Congress was increasing skeptical of the conflict in the face of human rights abuses, suggesting that Duarte may have become more important over the course of the conflict.

center of gravity shifted over time from ESAF in general to the newly created rapid-response battalions, which allowed the U.S.–El Salvador alliance to take the "strategic offensive." The FMLN's guerrilla forces were that group's principal means of seeking power. Initially, these forces were able to operate as battalion formations, but as ESAF's capacity grew, the FMLN guerrilla forces were forced to shift to traditional small-unit tactics.

Critical Capabilities, Requirements, and Vulnerabilities

ESAF and the FMLN both sought to conduct conventional offensives; this was the critical capability for both. As the conflict matured, the belligerents' critical capabilities shifted: The U.S. advisory teams assisted ESAF in slowly shifting toward counterinsurgency techniques, while the FMLN shifted to guerrilla tactics to avoid being decisively engaged. Throughout the conflict, the FMLN shifted from guerrilla to mobile warfare as conditions allowed.

To be capable of effectively executing critical capabilities, the United States needed to ensure that ESAF had access to required material resources (e.g., money and arms), training, recruits, and tactical intelligence. The United States was able to provide some resources through security assistance and training at the brigade-level through "operations, plans, and training teams," staffed chiefly by special forces personnel, and facilities, such as those at Ft. Bragg and at the regional training site in Honduras. Recruits and information were drawn from the population. ESAF appeared to regularly and coercively conscript soldiers, which reduced their need to develop a positive relationship with the rural population. This placed limits on the level of professionalization the military could achieve and reinforced the officer corps' opposition to the creation of a noncommissioned officer corps.

The FMLN also required recruits, operational security, and material resources, in addition to sanctuaries from which it could safely operate. Recruits and partial operational security (information denied to the government) were drawn from the people, material resources were provided by Cuba and Nicaragua (made possible by their Soviet sponsorship), and sanctuary was provided by the mountainous border with Honduras.

At a general level, for ESAF and the FMLN, these are all critical requirements, but whether the specific means by which they were met were critical requires an examination of whether alternative means were both available and would have allowed the belligerents to continue the conflict in its current form or pursue it in a different one (e.g., from guerrilla warfare to terrorism).

U.S. support to ESAF's access to resources and training was contingent on the force's opposition to communism (a Regan administration requirement), constraints on ESAF's human rights abuses, and some level of political reform (a U.S. congressional requirement). ESAF's access to the recruits was somewhat dependent on popular support, though there is no evidence that this ever presented a particular constraint. Access to operationally relevant information also depended on popular support, but, in this case, it seems likely that discontent with the feudal structure of El Salvador's society and the widespread abuse and even murder of civilians undermined ESAF legitimacy. The force's legitimacy as a servant of El Salvador's people constituted a vulnerability.

The FMLN depended on the population for recruits, and popular support was contingent on the perception that the FMLN was reformist. As with ESAF, the entire population did not need to see FMLN as legitimate—simply, 12,000 out of 5 million people had to be motivated enough to fight,[19] though clearly more were required as enablers (auxiliaries and underground) and more still were required to passively deny information to the government. The perception of FMLN legitimacy was vulnerable to increases in government legitimacy through political and military reform efforts. The FMLN's access to material resources was dependent on the support of Cuba and Nicaragua and, indirectly, on Soviet support to those regimes. FMLN dependence on Honduras's inaccessible terrain for sanctuary did not represent a vulnerability, since Honduras, though a U.S. ally, was unable to effectively drive out the fighters.

---

[19] Insurgents—and conventional forces—fight for many reasons beyond the perceived legitimacy of their cause. Research shows, however, that forces that have an ideologically dedicated leadership fight more effectively (Tompkins and Bos, 2013).

Decisive Points

In retrospect, there are only two clear decisive points in this conflict: San Salvador and the final peace negotiations. Had the 1981 "final offensive" successfully taken San Salvador, the conflict may not have concluded, but it would have fundamentally changed. It is possible that the United States would have found itself conducting an unconventional war similar to the one in Nicaragua. The final peace negotiations were the only truly decisive event over the course of the conflict—and that was contingent on the collapse of the Soviet Union ending the Cold War.

There were two functional military decisive points. The first was the U.S. effort to assist ESAF's partial transition from a barracks force to a field army; the second was the force's partial transition to a counterinsurgency force. The first decisive point was successfully reached when ESAF transitioned from being a barracks force to one capable of effective offensive operations (e.g., via the formation of the rapid response battalions), while the second decisive point was only partially reached because ESAF only partially transitioned to a counterinsurgency force. The first decisive point for the FMLN was its early transition from guerrilla tactics to mobile warfare. Its second decisive point was, as ESAF capacity grew, the successful transition back to a traditional guerrilla force.

In the competition for support of the population and international patrons, El Salvador's elections were another likely decisive point for the United States. Successful elections increased the legitimacy of El Salvador's democratic credentials, creating an environment in which both the domestic population and U.S. politics enabled increased support to the El Salvador.

Lines of Operation and Effort

U.S.–El Salvador lines of operation were as follows:

1. Destroy the FMLN force.
   - Consisted of principally ESAF conventional, battalion-sized assaults, with some recourse to small-unit counterinsurgency.

2. Control the population (excluding efforts that were human rights violations).
   - Efforts here included political (elections), development (civil action programs), and security (civil defense). There were some judicial and land reform efforts, but they were largely ineffective or even irrelevant as El Salvador's socioeconomic structure shifted. U.S. advisers' efforts to improve the military's treatment of the population also served to increase the legitimacy of the host nation, though they had limited success. ESAF forcibly conscribed youth as needed.
3. Deny FMLN geographic sanctuary.
   - A "hammer-and-anvil" approach was taken in cooperation with Honduras, but the mountains were too inaccessible to effectively pursue the FMLN.
4. Deny FMLN international support.
   - The United States conducted unconventional warfare in Nicaragua through the Contras. Concurrent U.S. efforts to "win" the Cold War played a role in the collapse of the Soviet Union, ultimately robbing the FMLN of its patrons' resources.
5. Increase ESAF capacity and capability.
   - U.S. efforts initially focused on rapidly modernizing and expanding the size of El Salvador's army. As the immediate threat that the FMLN posed to the incumbent regime declined and the group shifted from a mobile to a guerrilla campaign, there was a greater focus on helping ESAF become a competent counterinsurgency force. Among other things, U.S. trainers emphasized respect for human rights. Although improvement appears to have been modest, this progress was critical to preserving U.S. congressional support for the effort.
6. Diplomacy.
   - Both President Duarte and, later, President Alfredo Cristiani favored a negotiated settlement with the FMLN over a continuation of the conflict. Cristiani had sufficient influence among conservatives in his legislature to credibly deliver on negotiated promises with the FMLN.

Villalobos described the elements of FMLN strategy as

- the FMLN's offensive
- the insurrectional process of the masses in both the cities and the countryside
- generalized repression (presumably provocation of indiscriminate government repression)
- political disintegration of the government and the armed forces
- weakening of U.S. policies and its instruments in El Salvador.[20]

Based on review of the conflict, we characterize the FMLN's lines of operation as follows:

1. Take San Salvador/hold San Salvador at risk.
   - Taking San Salvador and other urban centers was a major goal of the "final offensive," though later urban assaults were likely more a negotiation tactic than an authentic effort to take the capital. This assault was also designed to act as a focal point to generate a popular insurrection against the government (i.e., the focoist approach), and the FMLN hoped to recruit the population as an operational center of gravity for employment against the regime. The popular insurrection failed to materialize.
2. Control the population.
   - Although El Salvador's rural population had substantial levels of hostility for the government, which it saw as oligarchic and abusive, neither did it have much interest in communist ideology. The FMLN was able to win support chiefly through the delivery of practical, immediate benefits. It was also able to deny legitimacy to the government by effectively communicating the military's abuses. Villalobos saw the military and political efforts (here, we treat them as information operations) as complementary. Sabotage served to further reduce the legiti-

---

[20] Tompkins and Crossett, 2012.

macy of El Salvador's government, though this typically back-fired and undermined FMLN legitimacy.

3.   Sustain FMLN capacity.
  – The FMLN's access to arms was largely dependent on the support of Cuba and Nicaragua and, indirectly, on Soviet support to those regimes. The significance of this support is underscored by the observation that the FMLN's leadership structure was in part conditioned on what factions had the greatest access to Cuban and Nicaraguan support. Maintaining that support required remaining credible agents of the communist revolution, in terms of ideological alignment and some modest level of political and military efficacy. All of this was premised on the continuing ability of Cuba, Nicaragua, and, ultimately, the Soviet Union, to support the FMLN's enterprise.

4.   Deny El Salvador international support.
  – The FMLN used El Salvador's economic inequality and human rights abuses to increase its own international legitimacy and to undermine the international legitimacy of El Salvador's government, which had enabled the United States to provide it military and economic aid. The development of international networks of sympathizers in the communist and democratic spheres greatly facilitated these efforts.

5.   Diplomacy.
  – As the conflict dragged on and international sponsorship declined (e.g., after election of a conservative president in Nicaragua in 1991), the FMLN increasingly viewed a negotiated settlement favorably. More broadly, the FMLN conducted an aggressive international information operations campaign, helping to bolster the sustainability of its cause.

Observations on Operational Art

The El Salvador case study illuminates both continuities and discontinuities between the practice of operational art in special warfare and its practice in conventional conflict (see Figure 5.1). In conventional warfare, operational art's decisive points are generally identified by examining enemy and friendly forces in relation to what are typically phys-

Figure 5.1
Special Warfare Operational Art in El Salvador

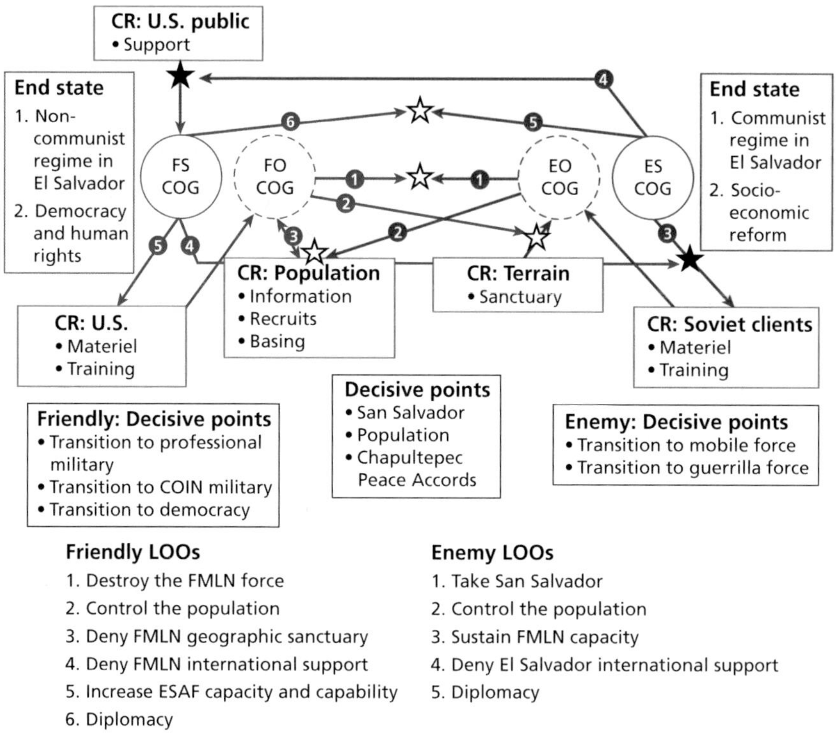

NOTES: COG = center of gravity. COIN = counterinsurgency. CR = critical requirement.
EO = enemy operational. ES = enemy strategic. FO = friendly operational.
FS = friendly strategic. LOC = line of communication. LOO = line of operation.
Stars = decisive points. Black stars = decisive points at critical vulnerabilities. Blue
numbers correspond to friendly lines of operation, red numbers to enemy lines of
operation. Critical requirements are grouped according to the source of the critical
requirement (e.g., population, terrain). Dashed circles indicate a nascent center of
gravity that must be mobilized rather than simply deployed.
RAND RR779-5.1

ical critical requirements and, perhaps, the seat of national political
authority (e.g., the capital). In special warfare operational art, decisive
points are identified by examining enemy and friendly forces in relation to a broader set of critical requirements derived from the population and international sponsors.

So, for example, while the FMLN initially sought a focoist victory through mobile warfare that aimed to inspire a popular insurrection, it effectively managed to adapt to a more classic Maoist protracted conflict using guerrilla tactics and back to mobile warfare as opportunity permitted. The group effectively integrated its military operations with a political strategy designed to delegitimize El Salvador's government domestically and internationally by publicizing its substantial human rights abuses, as well as through promises of socioeconomic reform made credible through the provision of services in rural peasant communities. Ultimately, however, the FMLN's desired end state, communist rule, was unappealing to the people of El Salvador.

El Salvador's government sought to defeat the insurgents militarily while bolstering its own domestic and international legitimacy through democratic elections and a broad suite of military, economic, and judicial reforms. It was ineffective in delivering on any of the reforms except for an increase in military effectiveness, but sufficient progress was made to sustain the support of its key patron, the United States. The military eventually shifted to some degree from conventional, multibattalion assaults to employing counterinsurgency techniques, including local security forces, civil action programs, and small-unit patrols.

U.S. operational art consisted largely of preserving and strengthening El Salvador's operational center of gravity—its army—and attempting to improve ESAF's access to critical requirements (e.g., legitimacy and information) held by the population. This was accomplished by protecting ESAF access to a critical requirement, U.S. materiel and training support, and attempting to drive a broad range of socioeconomic, political, and military reforms. Although progress was limited, reform efforts created political space in Congress for continued support to El Salvador. The United States sought to improve ESAF's access to additional critical requirements held by the population (e.g., information) through the adoption of counterinsurgency techniques, but this effort also met with limited success. Ultimately, increasing ESAF capacity to the point at which it would not lose outright to the FMLN and could restrain the group to guerrilla activities was sufficient to preserve core U.S. interests without drawing the United States into a costly direct counterinsurgency effort, as occurred in Vietnam. Perseverance was not merely a tactical virtue but also a strategic one. Political constraints and limited direct stakes prevented the United States from seeking to do itself what its partners could not. As a result, when both sides reached their culminating point, a sustainable negotiated settlement was reached.

The overarching narratives each side chose to employ, and how those narratives were realized through operations and programmatic reforms, had critical effects on outcomes. The FMLN's communist ideology severely limited its broader appeal across critical elements of El Salvador's society, even while its tactical activities won it important support among the peasant class and international civil society (later undermined by its employment of indiscriminate violence). The U.S.– El Salvador democratization agenda sustained and, in some cases, won important international backing, but El Salvador's tactical actions undermined it among the peasant class and jeopardized its international support. The FMLN was limited by a narrative scoped to a relatively narrow audience and declined in relevance as the conflict drove demographic changes, but it was bolstered by the efficacy and alignment of tactical actions with its narrative (for example, FMLN representatives embedded in villages provided medical care and worked in fields). Meanwhile, the government of El Salvador was bolstered by its attractive narrative and underlying ideology but undercut itself through tactical actions that did not comport with its narrative.

Unconventional Warfare: Afghanistan, 1980s

Following the Soviet invasion in 1979, the mujahedeen insurgency in Afghanistan went on for ten years. In 1989, the Soviets withdrew their forces in exhaustion but left Afghanistan in the hands of their client, Mohammad Najibullah. Najibullah was able to remain in power— much to the surprise of the Pakistani Inter-Services Intelligence directorate (ISI) and CIA. While conducting direct counterinsurgency, the Soviets lost 15,000 soldiers. By working through a client, they were still able to secure their core interests at a modest price. From the Soviet perspective, this could be seen as a successful transition from a misguided counterinsurgency to a sufficient FID effort.

U.S. assistance to the mujahedeen escalated from $30 million in 1980 to $715 million in 1990, including the provision of Stinger portable surface-to-air missiles.[21] U.S. aid was largely indirect, funneled through Pakistan, which demanded billions more in military aid to participate in the Cold War. Later, the United States developed some unilateral relations with mujahedeen commanders it considered especially effective, such as Ahmad Shah Massoud, but who were excluded by Pakistan for ideological and strategic reasons. Saudi Arabia matched U.S. funding, while Pakistan provided sanctuary and training camps for the insurgents. During this time, an extensive dark network was developed to transport materiel, financing, and mujahedeen from the Middle East (and beyond) to the Afghan jihad.

Similarly to the El Salvador case, the United States saw its interest in this conflict as an opportunity to roll back communism, but the direct Soviet occupation of Afghanistan also presented Washington with an opportunity to inflict on the Soviet Union "their own Vietnam." In this regard, it succeeded. The war largely concluded for the United States when the Soviet Union collapsed in 1991, though this was not formalized until January 1, 1992, when the U.S. Secretary of State and Soviet Foreign Minister pledged to cease support for their clients in Afghanistan.

Conflict Narrative

Monarchs governed Afghanistan for much of the 20th century. Even the 1973 coup was led by a member of the Muhammadzai royal family, rooting the government's legitimacy "in traditional dynastic descent."[22] The Saur revolution of 1978 brought communist Afghan factions to power. In the aftermath, the People's Democratic Party of Afghanistan (PDPA) attempted to modernize Afghanistan along communist lines so rapidly that the Soviets urged it to exercise greater caution and

---

[21] Coll, 2004.

[22] Thomas Barfield, *Afghanistan: A Cultural and Political History*, Princeton, N.J.: Princeton University Press, 2010.

restraint. These transformative efforts provoked resistance and rebellion from tribal and religious leaders. The PDPA's inability to stabilize the situation, and Soviet paranoia that the party's leader was being recruited by the CIA, led to the Soviet invasion in 1979.[23] The Soviets replaced the head of the PDPA and rolled back many of the policies that had enraged much of rural Afghanistan (e.g., women's rights, land reform). Concurrently, they instituted a heavy military repression of the resistance, including indiscriminate bombing, land mines, and forced population movements, and deployed 111,000 soldiers. The overall intent was to give the impression of permanent and irreversible occupation and to break the insurgents' will.

The Soviets had invaded Hungary in 1956, crushing a rebellion in five days with 200,000 troops, killing 25,000 Hungarians and losing only 669 Soviet soldiers. In 1968, the crackdown on Czechoslovakia cost the Soviets only 96 deaths.[24] Although the initial *coup de main* in Kabul successfully followed this model, the post–regime change environment proved the true challenge to Soviet strategic objectives. The Afghanistan adventure cost the Soviets more than 15,000 soldiers.

The Soviet invasion consolidated the insurgency, transforming it from a widespread local phenomenon into a national one. The Afghan Islamists in Pakistan were able to gain control over the insurgency in part because of their access to Saudi and U.S. resources through the offices of Pakistan's ISI.[25] Each of the parties contributing to the unconventional warfare effort in Afghanistan had distinct objectives.

---

[23] The Soviet coup de main model is worth greater study as a model of transition from FID to unconventional warfare. Major components include the pre-invasion insertion of KGB and Soviet military advisers down to the PDPA's battalion level, extensive precrisis reconnaissance, and ethnically appropriate Spetsnaz integration into the presidential security detail, all before the light armored airborne component actually invaded and proceeded to secure key nodes. See Lester W. Grau and Michael A. Gross, trans. and ed., *The Soviet-Afghan War: How a Superpower Fought and Lost*, Lawrence, Kan.: University Press of Kansas, 2002.

[24] David E. Johnson, Adam Grissom, and Olga Oliker, *In the Middle of the Fight: An Assessment of Medium-Armored Forces in Past Military Operations*, Santa Monica, Calif.: RAND Corporation, MG-709-A, 2008.

[25] President Carter signed a presidential finding directing the CIA to ship weapons to the mujahedeen in 1979.

As noted earlier, the United States sought to give the Soviet Union a costly, protracted insurgency to sap its resources, sow domestic discord, and dull its military readiness. As the insurgency matured and became politically popular in the United States, goals gradually shifted from "bleeding" the Soviets to defeating them. Saudi Arabia sought to bolster its Islamist credentials to placate domestic critics at a time when militant Islam was gaining importance in the Arab world. Pakistan's motives were more complex. It wanted to (1) exploit the United States as a patron in its competition with India, (2) preclude challenges to the Durand Line (the border between Pakistan and Afghanistan) by mobilizing Pashtuns on both sides in an anti-Soviet jihad, (3) keep the Soviets away from Pakistan's border to retain "strategic depth" vis-à-vis India, and (4) consolidate the Pakistani President Muhammad Zia-ul-Haq's Islamist political base (similar to the Saudis). Fear of a retaliatory Soviet invasion (or increased terrorism) led to take a very nuanced attitude toward the unconventional warfare effort: "The water in Afghanistan must boil at the right temperature."[26] Since it was chiefly through Pakistan that resources flowed, it was Pakistan that was positioned to shape who was strong and who was weak in the resistance,[27] and so it was that Pakistan's priorities shaped the conditions of the postwar period. According to Coll, "There was no American policy on Afghan politics at the time, only the de facto promotion of Pakistani goals."

The Afghans were fighting multiple, rural, ethnically based wars led by warlords. The fragmented resistance created opportunities for their patrons to play favorites but boded ill for the post-Soviet era. There were divisions between political leaders in Peshawar and field commanders in Afghanistan. Internally, Afghanistan was divided roughly into northern, western, southern, and eastern theaters. Ahmed Shah Massoud led the Tajiks in the north, Ishmail Khan led the west, and Pashtuns who supported Gulbuddin Hekmatyar held the east, while the south was fractured among multiple insurgent groups. "What all

---

[26] Coll, 2004.

[27] Ahmed Shah Massoud was sidelined by the ISI, but he was able to effectively support his own efforts through the recovery of Soviet materiel and, later, by direct outreach to Washington and other sponsors.

these parties and leaders had in common was the inordinate amount of time they spent just keeping their coalitions together."[28]

Insurgent tactics consisted largely of ambushes, raids, and harassing fires conducted by a few dozen to 350 insurgents, relying principally on small arms and mortars and recoilless rifles. Attacks on strong points could harness as many as 10,000 mujahedeen.[29] Ambushes and raids on Soviet and Democratic Republic of Afghanistan (DRA) lines of communication and isolated garrisons led to security force consolidation, successfully placing three-quarters of Soviet forces on the defensive. The insurgents also employed urban guerrilla tactics—assassination and sabotage—to degrade Soviet morale (already poor among conscripts) and increase the costs of occupation. This general approach to evicting occupiers had effectively served the Afghans since the time of Alexander the Great; as Barfield observed, "It was easier to come to an accommodation with such people than continually fight them, and most state powers chose that policy."[30]

The Soviets sought to suppress the insurgents through direct control of urban centers and "draining the sea" in which the insurgents swam by depopulating the countryside through force population removals, bombing communities, and mining fields.[31] During the Soviet occupation, the PDPA intelligence service grew to 30,000 professionals. The Soviets also attempted more politically sophisticated approaches, including playing tribes against one another and educating thousands of Afghan children in the Soviet Union.[32] Tactically, this had some effect, causing even Ahmed Shah Massoud to agree to cease attacking Soviet convoys for a time. But the insurgents used these lulls to reconstitute their strength and consolidate Afghan opposition to the Soviets.

---

[28] Barfield, 2010.

[29] Grau and Gross, 2002.

[30] Barfield, 2010.

[31] See Valentino, Huth, and Balch-Lindsay, 2004, on mass killings as part of counterinsurgency strategy.

[32] Scott R. McMichael, "The Soviet Army, Counterinsurgency, and the Afghan War," *Parameters*, Carlisle, Pa.: U.S. Army War College, 1989.

The Soviets also sought to seal the border to Pakistan, through which they knew manpower and materiel flowed to the insurgency. The Soviets employed heliborne Spetsnaz SOF and signals intelligence teams to identify and interdict insurgent movement on the border, supported by Mi-24D assault helicopter attacks. Although they inflicted heavy casualties on the mujahedeen, the effort was insufficient to close the border.

By 1986, the Soviets were committed to leaving Afghanistan; the domestic Soviet population was hostile to the continued prosecution of the war due to its financial cost and the toll on Soviet soldiers. The Soviets did not complete their military withdrawal until February 1989, and even then some covert advisers remained to assist Najibullah's security forces.

Once the Soviets left, Najibullah was able to undercut the narrative of jihad, highlighting that it was a conflict among Muslims. The ISI and CIA overplayed their hand, attempting to transition the insurgency too quickly to mobile warfare, resulting in a failed conventional-style assault on Sarobi Road in an effort to cut off Jalalabad from Kabul. The hope had been to take Jalalabad and announce a new mujahedeen-led government. Instead, the assault undercut the inevitability of Najibullah's fall. Using Soviet financial and military aid, and the Soviet withdrawal, Najibullah was able entice many of the mujahedeen to quit fighting, causing their numbers to drop from 85,000 in 1989 to 55,000 in 1990. Government-associated militia membership rose from tens of thousands to hundreds of thousands, while the formal military shrank from 400,000 in 1989 to 160,000 in 1991. Najibullah's strategy of political and military decentralization to regional warlords set the conditions for a sustainable regime that met the needs of many of Afghanistan's war powerbrokers and mujahedeen—if not the Afghan people themselves—so long as Soviet resources continued to flow.

Application of Operational Art
Belligerents' Conflicting End States
The Soviets initially invaded Afghanistan out of fear that it was about to tilt toward the West, perhaps becoming a staging location for U.S.

nuclear weapons.[33] The relatively modest goal of preventing Afghanistan from becoming a Western ally somehow expanded into a protracted counterinsurgency to stabilize the PDPA regime. By 1986, Gorbachev had concluded, "The strategic goal is to finish the war in one, maximum two years, and withdraw the troops."[34] The only other consideration was a desire to limit the spread of radical Islam. The PDPA's goal when it first seized power in Afghanistan was to modernize it. Following the Soviet invasion and a replacement of Afghanistan's leadership cadre, its goal narrowed to retaining power.

U.S. goals expanded from an initial desire to enmesh the Soviets in a protracted conflict to delivering the Soviets the embarrassment of a loss to the mujahedeen insurgents. Pakistan sought to establish a pro-Pakistan regime in Kabul, and Saudi Arabia sought to export its Islamist extremist problem.

Strategic Centers of Gravity

The Soviet-PDPA strategic center of gravity was the alliance's desire to prevent the Pakistan-U.S.-mujahedeen coalition from installing a new regime in Kabul. This was a relatively narrow strategic center of gravity from which to wage a war, but the limited objectives allowed the Soviets and the PDPA to display a remarkable amount of tactical flexibility in the long run. It did not, however, engage the passions of either the Soviet or Afghan people.

The U.S.-Pakistan-Saudi-mujahedeen strategic center of gravity was the moral fervor for the defeat of communism and the Soviets in Afghanistan. This anti-imperial crusade was an attractive enough narrative to attract the support of domestic audiences across the coalition. U.S. interests in the region were broader than this (e.g., growing Islamist anti-Americanism), but the strategic focus on rolling back communism accurately reflected U.S. priorities and allowed greater tactical flexibility.

---

[33] Coll, 2004.

[34] Coll, 2004, p. 158.

Operational Centers of Gravity

The Soviet-PDPA operational center of gravity was the Soviet military forces, since the PDPA's military was largely unwilling to conduct offensive operations. Arguably, the Spetsnaz-intelligence-assault helicopter teams and the conventional motorized infantry units constituted two separate operational centers of gravity.

The U.S.-Pakistan-Saudi-mujahedeen alliance had several operational centers of gravity, most prominently Hekmatyar's forces. Massoud and Ishamel Khan's forces constituted additional operational centers of gravity; as Tajiks, they were sidelined by Pakistan even as they clearly played important roles in the outcome of the conflict.

Critical Capabilities, Requirements, and Vulnerabilities

The Soviets sought to destroy the population's will and capacity to support the insurgency, to interdict manpower and materiel coming from Pakistan, and to directly attrit the mujahedeen forces. To do this, they required massed fires, armored and heliborne mobility, infantry to control population movements, civil affairs and information operations (e.g., communist education), and intelligence to drive raids on the Afghan-Pakistani border. The Soviets also sought to construct a PDPA operational center of gravity in the form of conventional military action, though they were largely unsuccessful. The mujahedeen and allies sought to attrit and demoralize the Soviets through guerrilla attacks (e.g., ambushes and raids) and subversion (e.g., assassination and sabotage). The U.S.-Pakistan-Saudi alliance needed to be able to run a covert logistics and financial network. For Pakistan's narrower interests, it needed to control the mujahedeen factions that benefited from its support.

For the Soviets to attrit insurgents, conduct intelligence-driven raids, and control population movements, they required the sustainment of their conventional military capabilities by Soviet soldiers, which, in turn, required some minimal level of indifference among the Soviet population and open lines of communication. The conduct of effective civil and information operations required access to information about what elements of the Afghan population were both critical to persuade and capable of (coercive) persuasion. To build an effective PDPA army, the Soviets also required manpower from the Afghan population. For the mujahedeen to conduct guerrilla attacks and subversion, they required intelligence on Soviet troop locations and movements from the Afghan population in urban and rural areas; weapons and training from the U.S.-Pakistan-Saudi network; sanctuary in Pakistan, in inaccessible terrain, or among the population; and access to manpower and sustainment provided (principally) by the Afghan population.

Critical vulnerabilities of the DRA forces included their ability to access and retain manpower from the population. The PDPA's narrative and actions promoting the communist modernization of Afghanistan were deeply alienating to most of the population. Insofar as these messages might have appealed to subpopulations (e.g., women's rights), the population in general did not have an organizational form for collective action and, being embedded in traditional Afghan social power structures, lacked the ability to mobilize even if it wished to. This vulnerability was mitigated as the Soviets withdrew and Najibullah shifted to a nationalist Islamist narrative, framing the mujahedeen as puppets of Pakistan, coupled with the devolution of power to regional warlords. Soviet vulnerabilities included dependence on long, thinly defended lines of communication and the tacit support of the Soviet people. Through attrition of Soviet forces (rather than information operations decrying imperialism to the Soviet population), the Afghans successfully, if inadvertently, exploited Soviet forces' dependence on Soviet public support. The Soviets sought to exploit mujahedeen dependence on external support and the population but found, to their frustration, that these relationships were not as vulnerable as expected. Although they were able to decimate Afghanistan's rural population, its will was not broken—at least not enough to effectively interdict the relatively thin requirements of the mujahedeen. U.S. public support did not constitute a vulnerability in this context, given that there was a strong narrative that resonated with U.S. anticommunist attitudes and principled support for self-determination.

Decisive Points

Geographic decisive points in the conflict included the Salang Tunnel between Afghanistan's Parwan and Baghlan provinces, the Pakistan border, Jalalabad, and Kabul. Had the mujahedeen been able to interdict the Salang Tunnel, the only north-south pass that remained usable year-round, or had the Soviets been able to interdict the mujahedeen's covert lines of communication running across the Pakistan border, each belligerent would have gained a marked advantage. For the mujahedeen, capturing Jalalabad would have created a sufficient impression of inevitability that they might have been able to retain the initiative and break Najibullah's grip on power before his loss of Soviet support. Ultimately, control of Kabul has always been the symbol of power, if not sovereignty, in Afghanistan, and its capture was the final objective of each of the mujahedeen factions.

Functional decisive points for the Soviets and the PDPA were the transition of the DRA military into a professional force capable of conducting effective offensive operations and Najibullah's successful transition to dependence on regional militias (though this dependence proved disastrous for Najibullah when the Soviet Union collapsed). For the mujahedeen, the successful transition from isolated acts of armed resistance to a set of organized guerrilla forces constituted one functional decisive point; a second was their unsuccessful transition to mobile warfare in the failed assault on Jalalabad. The ultimate decisive point was the collapse of the Soviet Union, Najibullah's sponsor, and the resultant collapse of his patronage networks.

Lines of Operation and Effort

The U.S.-mujahedeen lines of effort included the following:

1. Attrition and subversion of the Soviet-DRA military.
    - Attrition efforts consisted chiefly of small-unit ambushes and raids. Urban subversion efforts included sabotage and assassination to demoralize the Soviets and their Afghan collaborators. Ultimately, this effort undermined the Soviet public's support for the war effort, precipitating Gorbachev's decision to withdraw Soviet forces.

2.   Mobilization of the population.
   – The population was mobilized along multiple lines, ranging from religious to ethnic and tribal. Early on, this effort was directly assisted by PDPA's expansive modernization efforts running against the grain of Afghan culture and entrenched interests (e.g., women's rights, land reform) and, later, by heavy-handed Soviet depopulation tactics.
3.   Interdiction of Soviet-DRA military lines of communication.
   – The Soviet mechanized military was heavily dependent on logistical support to sustain its operations. Frequently, its lines of communication passed through heavily constricted terrain, allowing the Afghans to attack from the heights.
4.   Increase mujahedeen capacity and capability.
   – U.S.-Pakistan-Saudi efforts to increase mujahedeen capacity required the development of a covert logistics and financial network, as well as the mobilization of political support to supply it. The actual support consisted of small arms and money, but late in the conflict encompassed man-portable Stinger anti-air missiles. Pakistan attempted to use its position as the final link to the mujahedeen to shape the post-Soviet Afghan environment to meet its broader strategic aims.

The Soviet-DRA lines of effort included the following:

1.   Attrition of mujahedeen.
   – Early on, the Soviets conducted deliberate offensives, beginning with extensive preparatory indirect fires from fixed-wing aircraft, helicopters, artillery, and rockets, followed by an armored assault. Later, motorized rifle units were employed to secure major urban areas, lines of communication, and other key nodes; air assault and special operations units were used to conduct direct action missions against the insurgents.

2.   Depopulation of the mujahedeen's support areas.
   – "Destruction of the rural economy, genocidal razing of villages, forced resettlement, and the resulting creation of millions of refugees" were the results of the Soviets' strategy.[35]
3.   Selective Afghan modernization.
   – Without sufficient forces (even at a peak strength of 111,000) to subdue the insurgency, the Soviets emphasized controlling major urban areas and longer-term counterinsurgency efforts, including "political indoctrination . . . [and the] education of thousands of Afghan children in the Soviet Union."[36] In essence, it was the Soviets' "deep" battle in the counterinsurgency context.
4.   Interdict mujahedeen lines of communication along the Pakistan border.
   – One of the major missions the Soviets' direct-action units was the interdiction of mujahedeen lines of communication at the Pakistan border. Spetsnaz would attempt to conduct ambushes, with support from assault helicopters. Although this delayed the supply of mujahedeen forces, the border could not be decisively secured.
5.   Increase DRA military capacity and capability.
   – Although the Soviets were successful in increasing the size of the DRA military, they failed to transition it into an effective force capable of offensive operations. Local commanders would frequently achieve détente with their mujahedeen counterparts.

Observations on Operational Art

Like the El Salvador case study, the Afghan case highlights the importance in special warfare operational art of identifying decisive points by examining enemy and friendly forces in relation to critical requirements met by the population (e.g., manpower, information) and international sponsors (e.g., materiel, training). Also like the El Salvador case study, the employment of a compelling narrative sustained the

---

[35] McMichael, 1989.

[36] McMichael, 1989.

friendly strategic center of gravity (e.g., liberation, jihad) while degrading the enemy's (see Figure 5.2).

The Soviets attempted to conduct attrition warfare against both the people and the insurgents, while conducting a temporally "deep fight" in the human domain to modernize the urban centers they were

Figure 5.2
Special Warfare Operational Art in Afghanistan, 1980s

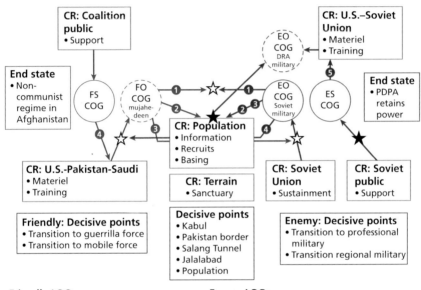

Friendly LOOs
1. Attrition and subversion of the Soviet-DRA military
2. Mobilize the population (e.g., Islam, tribe)
3. Interdict Soviet-DRA military LOCs
4. Increase mujahedeen capacity and capability

Enemy LOOs
1. Attrition of mujahedeen
2. Depopulate the mujahedeen's support areas
3. Selective Afghan modernization
4. Interdict mujahedeen LOCs at Pakistan border
5. Increase DRA military capacity and capability

NOTES: COG = center of gravity. CR = critical requirement. EO = enemy operational. ES = enemy strategic. FO = friendly operational. FS = friendly strategic. LOC = line of communication. LOO = line of operation. Stars = decisive points. Black stars = decisive points at critical vulnerabilities. Blue numbers correspond to friendly lines of operation, red numbers to enemy lines of operation. Critical requirements are grouped according to the source of the critical requirement (e.g., population, terrain). Dashed circles indicate a nascent center of gravity that must be mobilized rather than simply deployed.
RAND RR779-5.2

able to hold through propaganda and education. The inability (and insufficient interest) to win the "close fight" in the human domain (i.e., to gain the support of the Afghan population) led to the Soviets' inability to either develop an effective DRA military or cut off the mujahedeen from their base of support in Afghanistan. The forbidding terrain and porous nature of the Pakistan border also prevented the Soviets from effectively interdicting the critical mujahedeen lines of communication.

The mujahedeen were able to effectively deploy a compelling narrative that cemented support for their efforts among the Afghan people, in particular, and broad range of external sponsors. Islam, traditional values, and a historical repertoire of resistance to occupying powers proved a potent mix to help preserve the mujahedeen strategic center of gravity. The tribal organization of Pashtuns, in particular, provided a strong preexisting infrastructure of social networks on which to build an insurgency.

The U.S. operational art manifested in the construction of a coalition of external sponsors for the mujahedeen and the (somewhat) calculated escalation of the conflict as U.S. military leaders developed a better understanding of mujahedeen capabilities, Soviet counter-escalatory behavior, and the depth of U.S. domestic support for the effort. Pakistan's operational art may have been the most sophisticated. Rather than simply conducting unconventional warfare to drive out the Soviets, Pakistan selectively supported and excluded elements of the mujahedeen to shape favorable strategic conditions for the post-Soviet phase of the conflict. Although its favored client, Hekmatyar, was not able to seize power, the covert infrastructure that Pakistan constructed was later able to support the Taliban's rise to power, providing the strategic depth it sought.

Notional Scenario: Transition from Unconventional Warfare to Foreign Internal Defense

In this scenario, we review how an unconventional warfare campaign might be employed against an authoritarian regime in the U.S. Cen-

tral Command area of responsibility, with committed regional sponsors and allies, in support of a population that is initially pursuing
nonviolent resistance. Special warfare offers several approaches for supporting the protests and, later, armed resistance against the targeted
regime. Here, we illustrate a covert, primarily nonviolent unconventional warfare approach that branches into violent unconventional
warfare and, finally, transitions into FID. In Appendix E in the companion volume, we outline several additional scenarios.

Conflict Narrative

Prodemocracy demonstrations are held across an authoritarian country. The regime responds with a violent crackdown on the opposition.
The United States has several equities at stake, including humanitarian
concerns, democratic norms, the targeted regime's support to regional
terrorist groups, sectarian spillover effects on regional allies, and the
risk of Islamist control of the postregime state. U.S. intervention is
complicated by tensions between the state's majority religious group
(Sunni) and the minority religious group, which has historically supported the authoritarian regime (Shi'a); additional complications come
from the support to the regime from regional allies whose core interests
are closely tied to the survival of the authoritarian regime (asymmetry
of interests), the regime's control of chemical weapons, and divisions
within the resistance itself between moderates seeking democratization
and those seeking to establish an Islamist state. The level of desirable
U.S. involvement (size and scope) is limited by the U.S. public appetite
for new foreign commitments following the U.S. withdrawal from Iraq
and reduced presence in Afghanistan.

Given a decision to intervene, the United States is confronted by a
number of challenges: Who constitutes the evolving opposition? What
are their postwar aims? Would U.S. support be helpful, or would it
undermine the legitimacy of the opposition? Given limited (i.e., non-
existential) U.S. interests in the conflict, what modalities would be both
effective and limit the exposure of U.S. credibility in the event that
the requirements for outright opposition victory grow beyond what the
United States could accomplish without a sizable ground force? How
might the targeted regime and its external sponsors escalate support in

response to U.S. intervention (e.g., genocidal acts, support for global terrorism)? If the targeted regime collapsed, what mechanisms could be used to limit the proliferation of chemical weapon materiel to international terrorist organizations? Given continued sectarian tensions and opposition to a democratic state by former regime allies, if the targeted regime were to collapse, how could the country be stabilized? Special warfare operational art can help commanders and planners navigate this space.

In designing an effort that engages a variety of stakeholders, and leverages activities related to joint intelligence preparation of the operational environment and PE, the TSOC commander identifies the relevant actors (including friendly, enemy, indigenous, and foreign) and their beliefs, actions, options, objectives, and interrelationships. These factors are documented in narrative and visual form, initially in an open form but ultimately in refined form through center-of-gravity analysis. In several instances, the factor is uncertain and is described as such. These uncertainties would be appropriate for integration into the assessment process.

To facilitate the interpretation of the narrative, we list the relevant actors here:

- authoritarian regime
- the regime's military
- moderate opposition
- nonviolent resistance
- moderate armed opposition
- extremist opposition (associated with al Qaeda)
- the general population
- the Sunni population (associated with the opposition)
- the Shi'a population (associated with the regime)
- business
- the labor force
- regime state ally
- regime Shi'a violent extremist organization (VEO) ally
- the United States
- the joint force and other government agencies

- opposition regional state allies
- nongovernmental and intergovernmental organizations (e.g., UN, World Bank).

Operational Art
Belligerents' Conflicting End States

The targeted regime seeks to retain power, while minorities fear for their own security in a post-authoritarian state dominated by the majority religious group. The regime's regional state ally seeks to retain its influence in the targeted state, in part to retain the ability to supply arms to a hybrid terrorist group in a country neighboring the targeted regime. The hybrid VEO seeks to keep the authoritarian regime in power to avoid losing access to arms from its regional ally, which depends on lines of communication running through the contested state.

The largely Sunni opposition seeks to displace the current regime, but beyond that, the opposition is split between those seeking greater political freedom (the moderate opposition) and those seeking to replace the authoritarian Shi'a regime with a Sunni Islamic one (the extremist opposition). The extremist opposition has linked itself to al Qaeda. The United States and its regional allies seek the authoritarian regime's removal to reduce the influence of the regime's allies in the region and prevent the proliferation of weapons of mass destruction. U.S. allies are split between those wary of the role of jihadists in the insurgency and those who embrace any anti-regime partner.

If one of the opposition factions succeeds in overthrowing the authoritarian regime, the desired end states of the major actors would be unlikely to change significantly, with the victorious opposition faction seeking to consolidate its victory, the other opposition faction seeking to subvert it, and the elements of the former regime and its allies seeking to reverse it.

Strategic Centers of Gravity

The regime's strategic center of gravity is its alliance with its regional state and VEO allies and with the state's Shi'a population. This regime coalition is held together by the state allies' regional ambition, the

VEO's dependency, and Shi'a fear of a potentially vengeful Sunni majority.

The moderate opposition is only a loose coalition of groups held together by the goals of overthrowing the incumbent regime and accessing foreign assistance. The moderate armed opposition and nonviolent resistance movement, both operational centers of gravity, predated the moderate opposition's maturation as a national political movement, indicating the scope of their independence from centralized control. It may be too much to say that they are held together by democratic aspirations; many may be motivated by sectarian motives. The extremist opposition's strategic center of gravity is its alliance with al Qaeda, as well as the Islamist aspirations of its members. The extremist and moderate oppositions sometimes cooperate and sometimes conflict on the battlefield, indicating the very imperfect overlap of their respective strategic centers of gravity.

If the opposition is successful in overthrowing the regime, we would expect the factors holding the current regime coalition together to lead to the formation of an active Shi'a-based insurgency. In the language of operational art, the enemy's strategic center of gravity's continued—if altered—existence will result in efforts to mobilize a new operational center of gravity. There will likely be a window of opportunity for fracturing the altered strategic center of gravity following the transition to moderate opposition rule by integrating the Shi'a population into the new regime. The al Qaeda–affiliated extremist opposition would likely continue to fight its insurgency against the new moderate regime. The extremist opposition's desire to dominate the moderate opposition will likely take on more importance as victory over the authoritarian regime appears more certain.

Operational Centers of Gravity

The regime's operational center of gravity is its conventional army, though SOF and the navy also play a role in the counterinsurgency effort. The regional Shi'a VEO forces constitute a separate operational center of gravity for the regime's coalition. The regime's regional ally's SOF appear to be acting more as enablers than as a distinct operational center of gravity.

The moderate opposition's operational centers of gravity, as noted earlier, are the armed opposition and nonviolent resistance. The former is a guerrilla force, while the latter is a decentralized network for the coordination of nonviolent resistance—a form of underground resistance.

The extremist opposition is, itself, an operational center of gravity and at times is seen as the most tactically capable element of the insurgency.

Critical Capabilities, Requirements, and Vulnerabilities

The regime's military is employing "Hama rules,"[37] what we earlier referred to as "draining the sea," targeting population groups presumed to support the insurgents to cow them into submission. Although the regime sporadically employs chemical weapons, they are more efficient than critical. In general, the regime needs to be able to mass fires and enjoy both air and armored mobility. In some cases, the regime's military conducts division-sized operations.

The armed opposition is conducting mobile warfare, engaging in battles and intensive urban combat. Typically, its largest formations are battalion-sized. The nonviolent resistance organizes protests and strikes. The extremist opposition conducts both subversion and mobile warfare, sometimes overrunning regime army positions.

To sustain its military, the authoritarian regime requires loyalty and weapons and munitions provided by regional allies. Maintaining political dominance of the country requires control of the capital and the regime's political base in the predominantly Shi'a regions, along with, possibly, the support of the "crony capitalists" to sustain it financially. The regime-aligned Shi'a VEO requires lines of communication with its sponsor state.

The moderate armed opposition requires material support and training from their external supporters (regional U.S. allies) and recruits from within the country, principally from the Sunni population. The nonviolent opposition also requires training and support

---

[37] "Hama rules" is a reference to former Syrian President Hafez al-Assad's crackdown on the Sunni rebellion in Hama, leveling entire neighborhoods "like a parking lot" (Thomas L. Friedman, "The New Hama Rules," *New York Times*, August 2, 2011).

from external supporters (e.g., DoS) and a mobilized population to engage in nonviolent efforts. The extremist armed opposition requires training and material support from al Qaeda and recruits from the Sunni population.

The regime's dependence on crony capitalists, if it is dependence, could constitute a critical vulnerability. Its control of the Shi'a region is unlikely to slip, but if the opposition takes and holds the capital, it could place the regime in the position of retreating to a rump state. Furthermore, the ability of the regime's military to control territory would be greatly reduced if it lost air or ground mobility, either through the interdiction of ground lines of communication or the destruction of its air assets.

The Shi'a VEO's involvement in the contested state might be reduced if sectarian fighting with the politically marginalized Sunni broke out in its own host state. Stability at home is therefore a crucial vulnerability.

The moderate armed opposition needs to protect its access to international aid by foreswearing any association with al Qaeda or other jihadist movements and by regulating the behavior of its insurgents (e.g., no mass killings of minority groups). It also needs the support of the population, won through success on the battlefield against the regime.

The extremist opposition wins support from al Qaeda through its commitment to an Islamic state and from the population through its success on the battlefield.

If the moderate opposition succeeds in defeating the incumbent regime, the most important changes in critical factors likely involve the transition of sources of legitimacy for the opposition from success on the battlefield to the provision of security to the population, as well as from the construction of a governing coalition that ties together the critical segments of society, including the Shi'a.

Decisive Points

Geographic decisive points include the capital and the contested state's most populous cities. The support of the Sunni population, whether it goes to the moderate or extremist opposition or is cowed by the regime's military, is a functional decisive point. Whether the majority of the regime's military remains loyal to the regime is another decisive point. The support of the labor force (e.g., via strikes or sabotage) could be decisive if Sunni capitalists are the source of a critical regime requirement, such as financing for patronage networks. Since the latter assumption appears particularly fragile, it would be a priority within the assessment framework. Negotiations between the regime's regional allies and the United States constitute a final functional decisive point in the unconventional warfare phase, if the arms and diplomatic sanctuary provided by its allies are critical requirements.[38]

For the FID phase of the campaign (after the regime has been deposed), one decisive point would be a sensible transition and integration of elements of the armed resistance into a professional military and security services. (Libya offers a fine example of failure on that front.) Other decisive points would include the integration of Shi'a powerbrokers into the new regime (e.g., prioritizing reintegration over retribution or even justice) and protecting the Sunni population from terrorist and insurgent acts designed to keep the population polarized. In the longer term, securing borders (likely impossible in the short term without international intervention) and integrating society as a whole through a common ideological program that transcends sectarian divides (e.g., nationalism, democracy, development) would be important for lasting peace. While recent conflicts have demonstrated the difficulties of doing these things well, they are nonetheless decisive points.

Lines of Operation and Effort

This analysis leads to a reasonable set of lines of effort for the moderate opposition and attendant U.S. support, which might include the following:[39]

---

[38] By *diplomatic sanctuary*, we mean the role the regime's allies play in preventing consensus in the UN Security Council to execute more aggressive measures, either against the targeted regime directly or to protect population segments targeted by the regime. The lack of Security Council consensus significantly disrupts efforts to build an international coalition, as well as U.S. domestic support for a campaign against the targeted regime.

[39] Regarding a similar situation in Syria, in a July 19, 2013, letter to Senator Carl Levin, Chairman of the Joint Chiefs of Staff General Martin Dempsey laid out five military options:

1. Mobilize the population.
   – Mobilizing the population would not mean simply creating a positive perception of the moderate armed opposition to gain passive support from the population but, rather, motivating and organizing the population for action and developing a national governing body for the relatively unorganized opposition. Efforts to develop a national governing body would involve facilitating dialogue among emergent regional and local opposition leadership and helping to develop a coherent strategy to overthrow the regime. The nonviolent resistance would be a useful element to build on. During the early stages of the conflict, support to the nonviolent resistance should be covert to avoid delegitimizing it as a foreign proxy. During the early nonviolent phase of the conflict, a particular focus should be placed on mobilizing elements of the Shi'a community and the regime's military to undermine critical pillars of the regime. Once the conflict transitions to a violent phase (e.g., guerrilla warfare), sectarian communities will likely become too polarized for important elements of the Shi'a community to risk reprisals following the fall of the regime (though reasons remain for trying to set conditions for the FID phase). When regime soldiers are asked to shoot unarmed civilians, they are more likely to defect than after engaging in repeated fire fights with opposition elements in which either they or their friends are injured or killed.[40] This narrowing of the potential social base for the uprising is reason enough to seek to keep the con-

---

Train, advise, and assist the opposition; conduct limited standoff strikes; establish a no-fly zone; establish buffer zones; and control chemical weapons. Conventional invasion was not one of the options considered. Control of chemical weapons would likely require a greater commitment than simply assisting the insurgents in overthrowing the Assad regime. The buffer zone option has a humanitarian objective. The no-fly zone would seek to take from the Assad regime an important military advantage over the insurgents. Standoff strikes and assistance to the insurgents are military options but by themselves do not constitute a coherent effort to relate ways and means to ends.

[40] Erica Chenoweth and Kathleen Gallagher Cunningham, "Understanding Nonviolent Resistance: An Introduction," *Journal of Peace Research*, Vol. 50, No. 3, 2013.

flict in a nonviolent phase until either it spirals out of control or it becomes clear that the coalition cannot be broadened beyond its Sunni social base. Efforts to broaden the social base would require the elaboration of a nationalist ideology that encompasses all communities. Although there is an empirical basis for attempting to pursue nonviolent strategies, assessment processes need to be in place to help motivate transitions to other courses of action should planning assumptions fail.

2. Nonviolent urban protests.

    – Once mobilized, the nonviolent resistance might be used to coordinate mass protests and strikes in both the private and public sectors. The United States could provide these groups with resources to maintain a minimal social safety net for those least able to forgo work and trade, perhaps significantly expanding the number of people willing to participate. The goal of these efforts would be to (1) delegitimize the regime; (2) broaden the base of committed anti-regime resistance, whether for additional nonviolent action, transition into the armed opposition, or setting conditions for FID; and (3) peel off key regime supporters, including segments of the Shi'a and business community.[41]

3. Mobilize the armed opposition.

    – Concurrent with the nonviolent phase, the United States would covertly seek to develop relations with emergent militant factions of the opposition. Initial efforts would be focused on developing an understanding of militant factions, including vetting them for U.S. support. Long lead-time requirements, such as the development of human intelligence sources and nonstandard logistical networks, would also go into development during this nonviolent phase of the opposition. Once

---

[41] This is essentially a nonviolent version of NATO efforts to coerce Milosevic during the war in Kosovo by targeting the commercial interests of his core supporters (Ben Lambeth, *NATO's Air War for Kosovo: A Strategic and Operational Assessment*, Santa Monica, Calif.: RAND Corporation, MR-1365-AF, 2001). Given that Milosevic accepted NATO's terms to preserve his regime, it is reasonable to ask whether a similar coercion strategy could be effective against Assad, who is fighting to preserve his regime.

the opposition's transition to violence becomes clear, nonlethal aid could be used to map the distribution patterns of U.S. aid to enable additional vetting of potential partners. Once partners have been vetted, increasingly capable lethal aid could be provided in tranches, with each tranche providing another opportunity for network mapping and partner vetting. The aid would also become an occasion for embedding advisers (special forces or from other U.S. government agencies) at both the tactical and strategic levels to increase the efficacy of combat formations, help refine strategic planning, and help the United States understand and influence the capabilities and interests of its partners. Advisers might also play a role in facilitating the consolidation of the armed opposition as an organization with command-and-control characteristics rather than a brand name. Escalation of U.S. aid might be conditional on the consolidation of armed opposition elements under common command and control, their ability to manage radical elements, and windows of opportunity to depose the regime.

4. Protect the population.
    - The population is a source of critical requirements for the opposition, and one the authoritarian regime is prepared to target cut off opposition access to recruits and other resources. This critical requirement has to be protected both for humanitarian and pragmatic reasons, and that protection has to be expanded beyond the Sunni base of the opposition. Protection of minorities is an important part of the broader influence effort to undermine the solidarity of the social and economic basis for the regime's rule.

5. Destroy the army and (selectively) extremist forces.
    - Without external combat support (e.g., standoff strikes, close air support), destroying the regime's army is likely an overambitious objective in the short term. However, even if external support is limited to train, equip, and advise, the combination of attrition and defection could culminate in the army's disintegration. While the moderate armed opposition is developing internal legitimacy, U.S. support should remain covert. Once

the moderate armed opposition's internal legitimacy is established or some other legitimating trigger for escalation occurs (e.g., overt intervention by the regime's regional state or VEO allies), U.S. advisory support to the opposition could become overt, or the United States could use the moment to escalate to providing close air support to the insurgents. Risks of U.S. escalation to overt support include regime allies' employment of proxy forces against the U.S. diplomatic presence and allies in the region and increased security assistance through the provision of sophisticated integrated air defense systems.

— Risks of efforts to destroy the regime's army include the loss of control of chemical weapons to extremist elements. To mitigate this risk, special forces could team with selected elements of the opposition to secure chemical munitions facilities until they can be destroyed. Priority would be placed on major facilities and areas where the extremist opposition is active. This would constitute a major line of effort in its own right, requiring the integration of multiple capabilities from various agencies over time.

— In the early phases of the conflict, the extremist opposition would only be assaulted where it sought to displace moderate opposition forces. The principal counterextremist efforts would be to demonstrate and communicate moderate opposition success on the battlefield, develop and communicate a compelling nationalist ideological alternative to al Qaeda and the authoritarian regime, and develop intelligence sources on the extremist opposition. Elements of the extremist opposition might even be integrated into the moderate armed opposition (assuming the perception could be built that the war was going the moderates' way). This would avoid fatally splitting the resistance while also laying the groundwork for national integration after the regime's fall (though fragmentation would remain a likely challenge). If extremists escalate counter–moderate force efforts, the moderate opposition could shift from a focus on destroying the army to destroying the extremists and consolidating the armed opposition under its control. The risk of the latter course of action is that it creates a window of opportunity for the regime to destroy a divided opposition.

6. Diplomacy.
   - Diplomatic efforts would seek to stop regime allies from equipping and providing diplomatic support to the regime, as well as to broaden the base of regional and international support for overt U.S. intervention. U.S. diplomatic efforts would also seek to shape the direction of aid from regional partners to moderate elements in the opposition rather than to extremists.

The authoritarian regime and its supporters' lines of effort would likely include the following:

1. Destroy the armed opposition.
   - Destruction of the armed opposition would be a largely conventional enterprise, including division-sized and smaller operations, given the training and organization of the regime's conventional forces.
2. Interdict population support to the opposition.
   - Interdiction of support to the opposition would follow "Hama rules," deliberately targeting the civilian population in areas supportive of the opposition to intimidate the population into submission.[42] Extensive use of internal security forces could be expected, including police and domestic intelligence services. Chemical weapons would likely be reserved for last-ditch efforts to preserve the regime, if the regime either believed it was losing or sought to carve out a rump state.
3. Preserve minority and capitalist support.
   - The regime would use influence operations to frame the armed opposition as terrorists. It might point to the condition of Sunnis in post-Saddam Iraq to maintain minority and capitalist solidarity. "False-flag" terrorist operations (acts conducted by regime agents in such a way that they are attributed to the

---

[42] Friedman, 2011.

opposition) might maintain an atmosphere of fear and animosity toward the opposition.
4. Diplomacy.
    – Regime allies would seek to dissuade or delay U.S. intervention by framing it as a repeat of the deeply unpopular invasion of Iraq, denying the United States the imprimatur of a UN resolution and preventing it from benefiting from the legitimizing endorsement of regional allies.

Extremist opposition lines of operation would likely include the following:

1. Destroy the regime's army and the moderate armed opposition.
    – The extremist opposition's priority would be destroying the regime's army and, only secondarily, destroying the armed opposition. The lack of organizational integrity exhibited by the moderate opposition makes it an attractive target for piecemeal integration rather than outright destruction.
2. Mobilize Sunni support.
    – Mobilization of Sunni support could be achieved through success on the battlefield, exploiting Sunni political and Islamist aspirations. Extremists might also seek to build on lessons learned from the al Anbar Awakening, seeking to avoid creating new grievances among the population—at least until they have achieved a monopoly on political and military power.

Observations on Operational Art

In our notional intervention, the regime's operational art mirrored that of the earlier Soviet efforts in Afghanistan to "drain the sea" and attrite the armed opposition, but with the important difference that the regime has a "strategic minority" to provide it with an enduring social basis for continued support in some form (see Figure 5.3). Unlike the Soviets in Afghanistan, the survival of this authoritarian regime is at stake. Although it is conceivable that the regime could accept a negotiated withdrawal to a sectarian enclave, the opposition may not be inter-

Figure 5.3
Special Warfare Operational Art in a Notional Scenario

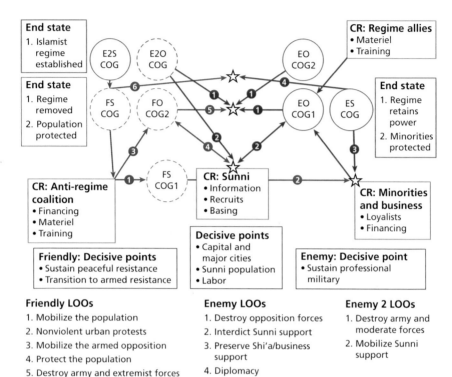

NOTES: In this scenario, "Enemy" is the regime, and "Enemy 2" is the extremist armed opposition. COG = center of gravity. CR = critical requirement. E2O = extremist armed opposition operational. E2S = extremist armed opposition strategic. EO = enemy operational. ES = enemy strategic. FO = friendly operational. FS = friendly strategic. LOC = line of communication. LOO = line of operation. Stars = decisive points. Blue numbers correspond to friendly lines of operation, red numbers to enemy lines of operation, and dark red numbers to extremist armed opposition lines of operation. Critical requirements are grouped according to the source of the critical requirement (e.g., population, terrain). Dashed circles indicate a nascent center of gravity that must be mobilized rather than simply deployed. FS COG1 = nonviolent opposition. FO COG2 = moderate armed opposition. EO COG1 = regime army. EO COG2 = VEO. E2O COG = extremist armed opposition.

RAND RR779-5.3

ested in or capable of credibly promising to permanently cede territory to the former regime.[43]

The moderate opposition's operational art consists of the simultaneous broadening and consolidation of a social base for the opposition that transcends its Sunni core while transitioning as necessary from a nonviolent protest movement to an armed opposition. The transition to armed opposition inherently risks polarizing the public along sectarian lines, but because of the lack of institutional integrity, it is unrealistic to expect nonviolent discipline to last indefinitely, and it may not be effective if the Shi'a community cannot be induced to join a countrywide revolt against the regime. Once the nonviolent phase has served the purpose of broadening the social base and further efforts are found to be ineffective, the opposition would make the deliberate transition to armed conflict.

U.S. operational art would consist in identifying inflection points (transitions) where discrete investments of support to the opposition might help overthrow the regime. Successfully identifying appropriate investments and windows of opportunity would require some presence on the ground to develop a sufficient understanding of potential partners' capabilities and objectives and to develop a sufficiently sophisticated understanding of the political relations among different opposition and regime factions. This situational understanding could then be exploited to mobilize the moderate opposition's strategic and operational centers of gravity through training, advisory, and other influence efforts. U.S. escalation (e.g., from nonlethal to lethal aid, from advisory support to close air support) could be managed to exploit windows of opportunity created by the adversary's own escalatory behavior (e.g., direct VEO intervention, the use of chemical weapons on civilians) while retaining the option of walking away if requirements outstrip the value of objectives. The latter would require an in-depth discussion with policymakers to understand the structure of U.S. escalation thresholds and at what levels of commitment to the conflict the credibility of U.S. forces become a stake in its outcome.

---

[43] For instance, the regime might fear that once the opposition had consolidated control over the capital and the remainder of the country, the new regime would have strong incentives (e.g., prestige, nationalism) to invade the promised safe haven.

CHAPTER SIX

Conclusions and Recommendations

Policymakers managing a constantly shifting security environment (e.g., Ukraine, the Islamic State) require more coercive options than the threat of conventional or precision-strike campaigns. Special warfare, as discussed in the preceding chapters, provides those options. However, simply exercising special operations capabilities in a reactive way is unlikely to secure strategic interests. Deeper thinking about strategic and operational art in special warfare is required in the national security community.

SOF operations have matured in recent years, as demonstrated by the success and expansive responsibilities of SOF commands in Afghanistan, the Philippines, and other theaters. These operations make evident the need to plan and execute special warfare campaigns in support of operational-level headquarters, conventional joint task forces, and TSOCs. SOF campaign planners need to be able to apply operational-level approaches, not only to lethal operations but also in the integration of capacity building, civil affairs, and other indirect approaches that are playing an increasingly important role in SOF operational planning across the globe. The blending of direct and indirect approaches will be a critical aspect of future campaigns.

Special warfare's unique contribution to operational art lies in the mobilization of partners' strategic and operational centers of gravity, and the neutralization or integration of the enemy's, in the human domain. Special warfare's contribution to operational art must be understood in the context of the competition with an adaptive adversary, rather than in terms of an exclusive focus on mobilization. Each conflict and mission is unique, and the population will not always be the center of gravity.

In many cases, the current doctrinal campaign model developed for large conventional-force operations—beginning with the "shaping" phase (peacetime activities), culminating with "dominate" (major combat operations), and moving through "stabilize" on its return to shaping—does not apply to special warfare.[1] The doctrine itself acknowledges that this joint campaign phasing model is not intended to be prescriptive, but it is symptomatic of joint planning culture. When the United States seeks to achieve its goals through special warfare it will, unsurprisingly, require a different conceptual model for the campaign. This is because special warfare works principally through local actors, employs political warfare methods, and requires the integration of a much broader suite of U.S. government agency capabilities (e.g., economic sanctions) than is typically envisioned in conventional campaigns.

Special warfare is not purely a shaping effort—implying an effort to either prevent or set the conditions for success in conflict—nor is it purely a supporting effort to traditional conventional campaigns. Special warfare can be a way of achieving strategic goals. Given current trends in security threats to the United States and its interests, special warfare may often be the most appropriate instrument of U.S. policy. As a result, the U.S. national security community needs to begin thinking seriously about special warfare capabilities and authorities, strategic- and operational-level plans, and operational art.

Recommendations

Providing policymakers with a credible special warfare campaign capability requires a variety of efforts by the institutional military, operational forces, geographic combatant commands, and policymakers.

---

[1]   The full joint campaign phasing model in JP 5-0 is shape (phase 0), deter (phase 1), seize the initiative (phase 2), dominate (phase 3), stabilize (phase 4), and enable civil authority (phase 5) (U.S. Joint Chiefs of Staff, 2011a).

The following recommendations should facilitate the development of a common intellectual framework for thinking about special warfare, and making related strategic, operational, and investment decisions. We begin by identifying each problem and its root cause.

Educating Planners: Strengthen Special Warfare Strategic and Operational Planning Capabilities

DoD special warfare planning capabilities are immature. A high-priority country plan reviewed for this study revealed important misunderstandings of the elements of campaign design, such as distinctions between strategic and operational centers of gravity and between centers of gravity and critical requirements. These distinctions are more than academic when they facilitate a propensity to start with a preferred target list and plan backward from there. A target list is not a strategy, and treating it as such risks encouraging the default employment of capabilities organic to the planner's organization, rather than critical thought regarding how a joint or interagency approach might be employed to secure U.S. interests or how host-nation nonmilitary capabilities might be leveraged.

Furthermore, special warfare campaign planners are not actively managed, and conventional planners receive limited exposure to special warfare planning challenges. Several SOF graduates of the Army's premier campaign planning school, the School of Advanced Military Studies at Fort Leavenworth, noted that enrollment was not encouraged and that prolonged separation from special forces groups generated significant career risk. A TSOC tour while still a major may be an important developmental experience for SOF campaign planners following graduation from the school (or after an intervening group tour). The John F. Kennedy Special Warfare Center and School's Unconventional Warfare Operational Design Course and the Special Operations, Operational Art Module, associated with the School of Advanced Military Studies are steps in the right direction but would likely benefit from greater joint, TSOC, and interagency engagement and influence. Currently, there appears to be no structured path for building special warfare strategists, for instance, through the U.S. Army War College's

Basic Strategic Arts Program coupled with additional special warfare–specific education.

Strengthening U.S. special warfare strategic and operational planning capabilities will require improvements in the education, professional development, and career management of the special warfare planners on whose expertise these campaigns will depend. DoD should develop a viable career track for campaign planners and strategists from within the SOF community, building on best practices from the conventional military planning community but also building special warfare–unique expertise. The health of this career track will require senior leader attention and monitoring within the SOF community (e.g., of promotion rates, utilization tour trends, and active debates in the professional literature). Creating a professional association for special warfare campaign planners and strategists would be a useful aid to foster both professional standards and innovation.

Educating Joint Organizations: Develop a Special Warfare Planning Culture

In recent special warfare planning efforts, there has been insufficient collaboration between SOF and conventional planners. SOF rarely have all the organic capabilities required for a campaign and will frequently fall under a joint task force, making the development of a joint special warfare planning culture critical. Special warfare campaigns are inherently joint, yet SOF and conventional forces lack a common understanding of special warfare and operational art.

Creating a joint special warfare planning culture will require the education of planners and commanders in the combatant commands, the Office of the Secretary of Defense, the Joint Staff, and the military services about the strengths, limits, and requirements of special warfare. Such a planning culture should include enhanced norms governing how operational objectives relate to policy objectives, assessments that are clearly linked to the commander's theory of the campaign, an enhanced focus on campaign continuity and transition planning, and recognition that precrisis efforts to prevent conflict or set conditions for conflict resolution ("shaping" activities, in the joint lexicon) should be treated seriously as decisive campaigns. These shaping campaigns will have characteristics quite different from conventional campaigns. Gaps and tensions among joint, Army, and SOF doctrine will need to be resolved.

One of the great strengths of SOF is the deference paid to the greater situational awareness of commanders on the ground. However, guidance coming from deployed headquarters is sometimes so broad as to enable subordinate commanders to focus their tactical operations wherever they see fit, resulting in a lack of unity of effort and significant discontinuity across changes in command. If each unit is allowed to pursue its own priorities, even dramatic local successes are unlikely to amount to more than a series of disconnected tactical events. If special warfare campaigns are to be successful, they need strategic and operational focus.

Educating U.S. Government Stakeholders: Institutionalize Unified Action

A standard complaint among operational-level planners (e.g., combatant command and TSOC planners) is that they do not receive clear policy guidance. Seeking to design campaigns to achieve policy objectives without a clear understanding of what those policy objectives are can be a frustrating and potentially fruitless exercise.[2]

Policymakers understandably seek to understand the full import of their options, and to preserve their options for as long as possible, before committing themselves to a particular course of action. Special warfare commanders and planners should seek to help policymakers explore the implications of setting particular strategic objectives through the development of multiple options, including "off-ramps" (i.e., branches and sequels) that allow policymakers room to maneuver as conditions (and preferences) change. Policymakers, in turn, should recognize that the best way to preserve decision space is not always to defer decisions but, rather, to recognize when critical investments need to be made early on to preserve options for later.

Creating the conditions for the "unified action" of U.S. government stakeholders is critical to the conduct of special warfare, since

---

[2]   Rosa Brooks, "Obama vs. the Generals," *Politico*, November 2013.

many of the most important capabilities reside outside the military. Even more so than in the joint community, focused effort will be required to educate key stakeholders on the strengths, limits, and requirements of special warfare. Key stakeholders may include country team members, regional and country desk officers, and directors at DoS, the CIA, USAID, the National Security Council, and other organizations that may reside outside the U.S. government. During the development of specific campaigns, active engagement with policymakers will be crucial to developing the proper alignment of ends, ways, and means. Engagements with partner agencies and policymakers in times of crisis are unlikely to be successful unless foundational relationships have already been established.

Particular focus should be placed on creating an interagency mechanism for special warfare policy coordination, establishing a commonly acceptable assessment framework, and determining what constitutes adequate policy guidance.

Providing Special Warfare Options: Develop Capabilities to Prevail Among the People

Unity of effort behind the right strategy and plan is necessary but insufficient for the successful execution of a special warfare campaign. Theater commanders need access to the requisite capabilities for the campaign's execution. The last decade and a half of war in Afghanistan and Iraq has degraded the depth of regional and country expertise in the SOF community and, to a lesser extent, the functional expertise required for special warfare. There are several initiatives that the SOF community can undertake to enhance the credibility of special warfare options for addressing strategic dilemmas. New investments in people, organizations, and intellectual capital will need to be made.

Preparing for the next special warfare campaign will require some refocusing for the SOF generation that matured during the Iraq, Afghanistan, and global counterterrorism campaigns of the past decade and a half. Continued war-gaming and training exercises over a broader range of scenarios than those encountered in recent theaters will help commanders identify where organizational and doctrinal change is required.

To provide a mature capability appropriate for the execution of a special warfare campaign, the SOF community should consider establishing a general officer–level operational headquarters element, similar to the division or corps level of conventional units. During operations in Afghanistan, in particular, the breadth of responsibilities within the special operations community steadily drove up the requirement for a higher-echelon command-and-control organization. These responsibilities included SFA, direct action, the initiation and management of innovative programs (e.g., village stability operations), and the coordination of diverse SOF (e.g., special forces, civil affairs, military information support), multinational, and host-nation efforts. The SOF command-and-control architecture evolved in an ad hoc way over the course of more than a decade, and it inhibited commanders' ability to adequately participate in theater-level planning.

The core contribution of special warfare to operational art is the mobilization, neutralization, or integration of operational and strategic centers of gravity in the human domain ("among the people," in General Sir Rupert Smith's words).[3] Influence capabilities at the operational level will be critical for the conduct of special warfare campaigns. Influence activities at the operational level are insufficiently mature. Research and concept development beyond current military information support activities is required and should include the development of political warfare concepts. Applying influence concepts, and special warfare more generally, in a specific campaign will require more than the regional expertise developed in some parts of the SOF community, leading us to recommend enhanced country-level expertise for selected countries of strategic significance. This additional expertise should be organizationally buttressed by the creation of "green" and "white" intelligence capabilities for nonlethal targeting and analysis.

---

[3]   Smith, 2005.

References

Agee, Ryan C., and Maurice K. DuClos, *Why UW: Factoring in the Decision Point for Unconventional Warfare*, thesis, Monterey, Calif.: Naval Postgraduate School, December 2012.

Barfield, Thomas, *Afghanistan: A Cultural and Political History*, Princeton, N.J.: Princeton University Press, 2010.

Blaufarb, Douglas S., *Organizing and Managing Unconventional War in Laos, 1962–1970*, Santa Monica, Calif.: RAND Corporation, R-919-ARPA, January 1972. As of November 20, 2015:
http://www.rand.org/pubs/reports/R919.html

Brooks, Rosa, "Obama vs. the Generals," *Politico*, November 2013. As of November 20, 2015:
http://www.politico.com/magazine/story/2013/11/obama-vs-the-generals-99379_Page3.html

Celeski, Joseph D., *Political Warfare and Political Violence—War by Other Means*, unpublished manuscript, undated.

Celeski, Joseph D., Timothy S. Slemp, and John D. Jogerst, *An Introduction to Special Operations Power: Origins, Concepts and Application*, unpublished manuscript, 2013.

Chairman of the Joint Chiefs of Staff Instruction 3100.01B, *Joint Strategic Planning System*, Washington, D.C., December 12, 2008, current as of September 5, 2013.

Chenoweth, Erica, and Kathleen Gallagher Cunningham, "Understanding Nonviolent Resistance: An Introduction," *Journal of Peace Research*, Vol. 50, No. 3, 2013, pp. 271–276.

Childress, Michael, *The Effectiveness of U.S. Training Efforts in Internal Defense and Development: The Cases of El Salvador and Honduras*, Santa Monica, Calif.: RAND Corporation, MR-250-USDP, 1995. As of November 20, 2015:
http://www.rand.org/pubs/monograph_reports/MR250.html

Clausewitz, Carl von, *On War*, Michael Howard and Peter Paret, trans., Princeton, N.J.: Princeton University Press, 1984.

Cohen, Eliot A., *Supreme Command: Soldiers, Statesmen, and Leadership in Wartime*, New York: Anchor Books, 2003.

Coll, Steve, *Ghost Wars: The Secret History of the CIA, Afghanistan, and bin Laden, from the Soviet Invasion to September 11, 2011*, New York: Penguin Books, 2004.

Connable, Ben, *Embracing the Fog of War: Assessment and Metrics in Counterinsurgency*, Santa Monica, Calif.: RAND Corporation, MG-1086-DOD, 2012. As of November 20, 2015:
http://www.rand.org/pubs/monographs/MG1086.html

Crist, David, *The Twilight War: The Secret History of America's Thirty-Year Conflict with Iran*, New York: Penguin, 2013.

Daalder, Ivo, and Michael O'Hanlon, *Winning Ugly: NATO's War to Save Kosovo*, Washington, D.C.: Brookings Institution Press, 2000.

Dobbins, James, Laurel E. Miller, Stephanie Pezard, Christopher Chivvis, Julie E. Taylor, Keith Crane, Calin Trenkov-Wermuth, and Tewodaj Mengistu, *Overcoming Obstacles to Peace: Local Factors in Nation-Building*, Santa Monica, Calif.: RAND Corporation, RR-167-RC, 2013. As of November 20, 2015:
http://www.rand.org/pubs/research_reports/RR167.html

Downs, George W., and David M. Rocke, "Conflict, Agency, and Gambling for Resurrection: The Principal-Agent Problem Goes to War," *American Journal of Political Science*, Vol. 38, No. 2, May 1994, pp. 362–380.

Dubik, James M., "Operational Art in Counterinsurgency: A View from the Inside," *Report 5: Best Practices in Counterinsurgency*, Washington, D.C.: Institute for the Study of War, May 2012. As of August 2, 2013:
http://www.understandingwar.org/sites/default/files/OperationalArt_in_COIN_0.pdf

Dunigan, Molly, Dick Hoffmann, Peter Chalk, Brian Nichiporuk, and Paul DeLuca, *Characterizing and Exploring the Implications of Maritime Irregular Warfare*, Santa Monica, Calif.: RAND Corporation, MG-1127-NAVY, 2012. As of November 20, 2015:
http://www.rand.org/pubs/monographs/MG1127.html

Echevarria, Antulio J. II, "American Operational Art, 1917–2008," in John Olsen and Martin van Creveld, eds., *The Evolution of Operational Art*, New York: Oxford University Press, 2011.

Erwin, Marshall Curtis, *Covert Action: Legislative Background and Possible Policy Questions*, Washington, D.C.: Congressional Research Service, April 10, 2013.

Exum, Andrew, *Hizballah at War: A Military Assessment*, Policy Focus No. 63, Washington, D.C.: Washington Institute for Near East Policy, December 2006.

Friedman, Thomas L., "The New Hama Rules," *New York Times*, August 2, 2011.

Gompert, David, and Terrence Kelly, "Escalation Cause: How the Pentagon's New Strategy Could Trigger War with China," *Foreign Policy*, August 2, 2013. As of August 19, 2013:
http://www.foreignpolicy.com/articles/2013/08/02/
escalation_cause_air_sea_battle_china

Grau, Lester W., and Michael A. Gross, trans. and ed., *The Soviet-Afghan War: How a Superpower Fought and Lost,* Lawrence, Kan.: University Press of Kansas, 2002.

Gray, Colin S., *Explorations in Strategy*, Westport, Conn.: Praeger, 1998.

Grdovic, Mark, *A Leader's Handbook to Unconventional Warfare*, Publication 09-1, Ft. Bragg, N.C.: U.S. Army John F. Kennedy Special Warfare Center and School, November 2009.

———, "Developing a Common Understanding of Unconventional Warfare," *Joint Force Quarterly*, No. 57, 2nd Quarter 2010.

Haddick, Robert, "The Pentagon Needs a New Way of War," *War on the Rocks*, March 18, 2014. As of November 20, 2015:
http://warontherocks.com/2014/03/the-pentagon-needs-a-new-way-of-war/

Headquarters, U.S. Department of the Army, *Operations*, Field Manual 100-5, Washington, D.C., May 1986.

———, *Army Special Operations Forces Unconventional Warfare*, Field Manual 3-05.130, Washington, D.C., September 2008.

———, *Special Forces Unconventional Warfare*, Training Circular 18-01, January 28, 2011a.

———, *Foreign Internal Defense*, Field Manual 3-05.2, Washington, D.C., September 2011b.

———, *The Operations Process*, Army Doctrine Reference Publication 5-0, Washington, D.C., May 2012a.

———, *Unified Land Operations*, Army Doctrine Reference Publication 3-0, Washington, D.C., May 2012b.

———, *Special Operations*, Army Doctrine Publication 3-05, Washington, D.C., August 2012c.

———, *Special Operations*, Army Doctrine Reference Publication 3-05, Washington, D.C., August 2012d.

Headquarters, U.S. Department of the Army, and Headquarters, U.S. Marine Corps, *Insurgencies and Countering Insurgencies*, Field Manual 3-24/Marine Corps Warfighting Publication 3-33.5, Washington, D.C., May 2014.

Hoffmann, D., *Civil-Military Coordination in Afghanistan*, Combined Forces Special Operations Component Command–Afghanistan Commander's Initiative Group Information Paper, November 5, 2010.

Huntington, Samuel P., *The Soldier and the State: The Theory and Politics of Civil-Military Relations*, Cambridge, Mass.: Harvard University Press, 1985.

Johnson, David E., Adam Grissom, and Olga Oliker, *In the Middle of the Fight: An Assessment of Medium-Armored Forces in Past Military Operations,* Santa Monica, Calif.: RAND Corporation, MG-709-A, 2008. As of November 20, 2015:
http://www.rand.org/pubs/monographs/MG709.html

Johnson, David E., Michael Spirtas, and Ghassan Schbley, *Rediscovering the Full Range of Military Operations*, unpublished RAND Corporation research, 2009.

Johnson, Michael, *Strange Gravity: Toward a Unified Theory of Joint Warfighting*, Ft. Leavenworth, Kan.: School of Advanced Military Studies, U.S. Army Command and General Staff College, 2001.

Johnston, Patrick B., "Does Decapitation Work? Assessing the Effectiveness of Leadership Targeting in Counterinsurgency Campaigns," *International Security*, Vol. 36, No. 4, Spring 2012, pp. 47–79.

Jones, D., *Ending the Debate: Unconventional Warfare, Foreign Internal Defense, and Why Words Matter*, thesis, Ft. Leavenworth, Kan.: U.S. Army Command and General Staff College, 2006.

Jones, Seth G., Olga Oliker, Peter Chalk, C. Christine Fair, Rollie Lal, and James Dobbins, *Securing Tyrants or Fostering Reform? U.S. Internal Security Assistance to Repressive and Transitioning Regimes*, Santa Monica, Calif.: RAND Corporation, MG-550-OSI, 2006. As of November 20, 2015:
http://www.rand.org/pubs/monographs/MG550.html

Kelly, Justin, and Mike Brennan, *Alien: How Operational Art Devoured Strategy*, Carlisle, Pa.: Strategic Studies Institute, U.S. Army War College, September 2009. As of November 20, 2015:
http://www.strategicstudiesinstitute.army.mil/pdffiles/pub939.pdf

Kiras, James D., *Special Operations and Strategy: From World War II to the War on Terrorism*, New York: Routledge, 2006.

Knox, MacGregor, and Williamson Murray, eds., *The Dynamics of Military Revolution 1300–2050*, New York: Cambridge University Press, 2009.

Krause, Michael, and Cody Phillips, *Historical Perspectives of the Operational Art*, Ft. McNair, Washington, D.C.: U.S. Army Center of Military History, 2005.

Lambeth, Ben, *NATO's Air War for Kosovo: A Strategic and Operational Assessment*, Santa Monica, Calif.: RAND Corporation, MR-1365-AF, 2001. As of November 20, 2015:
http://www.rand.org/pubs/monograph_reports/MR1365.html

Larson, Eric, Richard E. Darilek, Daniel Gibran, Brian Nichiporuk, Amy Richardson, Lowell H. Schwartz, and Cathryn Quantic Thurston, *Foundations of Effective Influence Operations: A Framework for Enhancing Army Capabilities*, Santa Monica, Calif.: RAND Corporation, MG-654-A, 2009. As of November 20, 2015:
http://www.rand.org/pubs/monographs/MG654.html

Long, Austin, Stephanie Pezard, Bryce Loidolt, and Todd C. Helmus, *Locals Rule: Historical Lessons for Creating Local Defense Forces for Afghanistan and Beyond*, Santa Monica, Calif.: RAND Corporation, MG-1232-CFSOCC-A, 2012. As of November 20, 2015:
http://www.rand.org/pubs/monographs/MG1232.html

Lostumbo, Michael J., Michael J. McNerney, Eric Peltz, Derek Eaton, David R. Frelinger, Victoria A. Greenfield, John Halliday, Patrick Mills, Bruce R. Nardulli, Stacie L. Pettyjohn, Jerry M. Sollinger, and Stephen Worman, *Overseas Basing of U.S. Military Forces: An Assessment of Relative Costs and Strategic Benefits*, Santa Monica, Calif.: RAND Corporation, RR-201-OSD, 2013. As of November 20, 2015:
http://www.rand.org/pubs/research_reports/RR201.html

Luttwak, Edward N., "The Operational Level of War," *International Security*, Vol. 5, No. 3, Winter 1980–1981, pp. 61–79.

Lyall, Jason, Graeme Blair, and Kosuke Imai, "Explaining Support for Combatants During Wartime: A Survey Experiment in Afghanistan," *American Political Science Review*, Vol. 107, No. 4, November 2013, pp. 679–705.

Markopoulos, Matthew, *Collaboration and Multi-Stakeholder Dialogue: A Review of the Literature*, version 1.1, Gland, Switzerland: International Union for Conservation of Nature and Natural Resources, Forest Conservation Programme, March 2012.

Mazzetti, Mark, *The Way of the Knife: The CIA, a Secret Army, and a War at the Ends of the Earth*, New York: Penguin Books, 2013.

McDonough, James, "The Operational Art: Quo Vadis?" in Richard Hooker, Jr., ed., *Maneuver Warfare Anthology*, Novato, Calif.: Presidio Press, 1993.

McMichael, Scott R., "The Soviet Army, Counterinsurgency, and the Afghan War," *Parameters*, Carlisle, Pa.: U.S. Army War College, 1989, pp. 21–35. As of November 20, 2015:
http://www.dtic.mil/cgi-bin/GetTRDoc?AD=ADA529242

McRaven, ADM William H., "Posture Statement of Admiral William H. McRaven, USN, Commander, United States Special Operations Command, Before the 112th Congress, Senate Armed Services Committee," March 6, 2012.

Molinari, Robert J., *Carrots and Sticks: Questions for COCOMs Who Must Leverage National Power in Counter Insurgency Warfare*, thesis, Newport, R.I.: Naval War College, 2004.

Morgan, Forrest E., Karl P. Mueller, Evan S. Medeiros, Kevin L. Pollpeter, and Roger Cliff, *Dangerous Thresholds: Managing Escalation in the 21st Century*, Santa Monica, Calif.: RAND Corporation, MG-614-AF, 2008. As of November 20, 2015:
http://www.rand.org/pubs/monographs/MG614.html

Mueller, Karl P., Jeffrey Martini, and Thomas Hamilton, *Airpower Options for Syria: Assessing Objectives and Missions for Aerial Intervention*, Santa Monica, Calif.: RAND Corporation, RR-446-CMEPP, 2013. As of November 20, 2015:
http://www.rand.org/pubs/research_reports/RR446.html

National Intelligence Council, *Global Trends 2030: Alternative Worlds*, Washington, D.C., 2012. As of November 20, 2015:
http://www.dni.gov/files/documents/GlobalTrends_2030.pdf

Nye, Joseph S., *The Future of Power*, New York: PublicAffairs, 2011.

Office of the Deputy Assistant Secretary of Defense for Plans, *Theater Campaign Planning: Planners' Handbook,* version 1.0, Washington, D.C., February 2012.

Osburg, Jan, Christopher Paul, Lisa Saum-Manning, Dan Madden, and Leslie Adrienne Payne, *Assessing Locally Focused Stability Operations*, Santa Monica, Calif.: RAND Corporation, RR-387-A, 2014. As of November 20, 2015:
http://www.rand.org/pubs/research_reports/RR387.html

Palilonis, David C., *Operation Enduring Freedom—Philippines: A Demonstration of Economy of Force*, Newport, R.I.: U.S. Naval War College, May 2009.

Paul, Christopher, Colin P. Clarke, and Beth Grill, *Victory Has a Thousand Fathers: Sources of Success in Counterinsurgency*, Santa Monica, Calif.: RAND Corporation, MG-964-OSD, 2010. As of November 20, 2015:
http://www.rand.org/pubs/monographs/MG964.html

Paul, Christopher, Colin P. Clarke, Beth Grill, and Molly Dunigan, *Paths to Victory: Lessons from Modern Insurgencies,* Santa Monica, Calif.: RAND Corporation, RR-291/1-OSD, 2013. As of November 20, 2015:
http://www.rand.org/pubs/research_reports/RR291z1.html

Perez, Celestino, ed., *Addressing the Fog of COG: Perspective on the Center of Gravity in U.S. Military Doctrine*, Ft. Leavenworth, Kan.: Combat Studies Institute Press, 2012.

Persico, Joseph E., *Casey: The Lives and Secrets of William J. Casey: From OSS to the CIA*, New York: Penguin Books, 1991.

Petraeus, David H., "Multi-National Forces–Iraq: Charts to Accompany the Testimony of GEN David H. Petraeus," PowerPoint slides, April 8–9, 2008.

Public Law 108-375, National Defense Authorization Act for Fiscal Year 2005, October 28, 2004.

Public Law 109-163, National Defense Authorization Act for Fiscal Year 2006, January 6, 2006.

Public Law 111-84, National Defense Authorization Act for Fiscal Year 2010, October 28, 2009.

Public Law 112-10, Department of Defense and Full-Year Continuing Appropriations Act, April 15, 2011.

Public Law 112-81, National Defense Authorization Act for Fiscal Year 2012, December 31, 2011.

Rabasa, Angel, Steven Boraz, Peter Chalk, Kim Cragin, Theodore W. Karasik, Jennifer D. P. Moroney, Kevin A. O'Brien, and John E. Peters, *Ungoverned Territories: Understanding and Reducing Terrorism Risk,* Santa Monica, Calif.: RAND Corporation, MG-561-AF, 2007. As of November 20, 2015: http://www.rand.org/pubs/monographs/MG561.html

Ramsey, Robert D., *Advising Indigenous Forces: American Advisors in Korea, Vietnam, and El Salvador,* Global War on Terrorism Occasional Paper 18, Ft. Leavenworth, Kan.: Combat Studies Institute Press, 2006.

Rico, Antonieta, "New Training to Focus on Regionally Aligned Forces Concept," *Defense News,* October 23, 2013.

Rudgers, David F., "The Origins of Covert Action," *Journal of Contemporary History,* Vol. 35, No. 2, April 2000, pp. 249–262.

Schofield, Julian, and Reeta Tremblay, "Why Pakistan Failed: Tribal Focoism in Kashmir," *Small Wars and Insurgencies,* Vol. 19, No. 1, March 2008.

Serafino, Nina M., *Security Assistance Reform: "Section 1206" Background and Issues for Congress,* Washington, D.C.: Congressional Research Service, April 19, 2013.

———, *Global Security Contingency Fund: Summary and Issue Overview,* Washington, D.C.: Congressional Research Service, April 4, 2014.

Sheehan, Michael, Assistant Secretary of Defense for Special Operations and Low-Intensity Conflict, *Future Authorities That May Be Necessary for Special Operations Forces to Adequately Conduct Counterterrorism, Unconventional Warfare, and Irregular Warfare Missions: Report to Congress in Compliance with the Reporting Requirement Contained in Sub-Section (d) of Section 1203 of the National Defense Authorization Act for FY 2012 (P.L. 112-81),* January 11, 2013.

Shy, John, and John W. Collier, "Revolutionary War," in Peter Paret, Gordon A. Craig, and Felix Gilbert, eds., *Makers of Modern Strategy from Machiavelli to the Nuclear Age,* Princeton, N.J.: Princeton University Press, 1986.

Simpson, Emile, *War from the Ground Up: Twenty-First-Century Combat as Politics,* London: Hurst and Company, 2012.

Smith, Rupert, *The Utility of Force: The Art of War in the Modern World,* New York: Alfred A. Knopf, 2005.

Staniland, Paul, "Organizing Insurgency," *International Security*, Vol. 37, No. 1, Summer 2012, pp. 142–177.

Strange, Joe, "Centers of Gravity and Critical Vulnerabilities: Building on the Clausewitzian Foundation So That We May All Speak the Same Language," *Perspectives on Warfighting*, No. 4, 2nd ed., Quantico Va.: Marine Corps War College, 1996.

Sullivan, Gordon, "War in the Information Age," *Military Review*, Vol. 74, No. 4, April 1994, pp. 46–62.

Thomas, Jim, and Chris Dougherty, *Beyond the Ramparts: The Future of U.S. Special Operations Forces*, Washington, D.C.: Center for Strategic and Budgetary Assessments, 2013.

Tompkins, Paul J., Jr., "Planning Considerations for Unconventional Warfare," unpublished document, Ft. Bragg, N.C.: U.S. Army Special Operations Command, 2012.

———, ed., *Assessing Revolutionary and Insurgent Strategies: Casebook on Insurgency and Revolutionary Warfare, Volume I: 1933–1962*, rev. ed., Ft. Bragg, N.C.: U.S. Army Special Operations Command and Johns Hopkins University Applied Physics Laboratory National Security Analysis Department, January 25, 2013.

Tompkins, Paul J., Jr., and Nathan Bos, eds., *Assessing Revolutionary and Insurgent Strategies: Human Factor Considerations of Undergrounds in Insurgencies*, Ft. Bragg, N.C.: U.S. Army Special Operations Command and Johns Hopkins University Applied Physics Laboratory National Security Analysis Department, January 25, 2013.

Tompkins, Paul J., Jr., and Chuck Crossett, eds., *Assessing Revolutionary and Insurgent Strategies: Casebook on Insurgency and Revolutionary Warfare, Volume II: 1962–2009*, Ft. Bragg, N.C.: U.S. Army Special Operations Command and Johns Hopkins University Applied Physics Laboratory National Security Analysis Department, April 27, 2012.

Tompkins, Paul J., Jr., and Robert Leonhard, eds., *Assessing Revolutionary and Insurgent Strategies: Underground in Insurgent, Revolutionary, and Resistance Warfare*, 2nd ed., Ft. Bragg, N.C.: U.S. Army Special Operations Command and Johns Hopkins University Applied Physics Laboratory National Security Analysis Department, January 25, 2013.

Tompkins, Paul J., Jr., and Summer Newtown, eds., *Assessing Revolutionary and Insurgent Strategies: Irregular Warfare Annotated Bibliography*, Ft. Bragg, N.C.: U.S. Army Special Operations Command and Johns Hopkins University Applied Physics Laboratory National Security Analysis Department, June 2, 2011.

U.S. Army Special Operations Command, *ARSOF 2022: The Future Operation Environment*, Washington, D.C.: Headquarters, U.S. Department of the Army, undated.

U.S. Code, Title 10, Armed Forces, Section 127, Assistance in Combating Terrorism: Rewards.

U.S. Code, Title 10, Armed Forces, Section 166a, Combatant Commander Initiative Fund.

U.S. Code, Title 10, Armed Forces, Section 166b, Combatant Commands: Funding for Combating Terrorism Readiness Initiatives.

U.S. Code, Title 10, Armed Forces, Section 167, Unified Combatant Command for Special Operations Forces.

U.S. Code, Title 10, Armed Forces, Section 2011, Special Operations Forces: Training with Friendly Foreign Forces.

U.S. Code, Title 50, War and National Defense, Section 3093e, "Covert Action" Defined.

U.S. Department of Defense, *Fiscal Year 2009 Budget Request Summary Justification*, Washington, D.C., February 4, 2008.

———, *Sustaining U.S. Global Leadership: Priorities for 21st Century Defense*, Washington, D.C., January 2012.

U.S. Department of Defense Directive 3000.07, *Irregular Warfare (IW)*, December 1, 2008.

U.S. Joint Chiefs of Staff, *Foreign Internal Defense,* Joint Publication 3-22, Washington, D.C., July 12, 2010.

———, *Joint Operation Planning,* Joint Publication 5-0, Washington, D.C., August 11, 2011a.

———, *Joint Operations,* Joint Publication 3-0, Washington, D.C., August 11, 2011b.

———, *Joint Task Force Headquarters,* Joint Publication 3-33, Washington, D.C., July 30, 2012.

———, *Special Operations,* Joint Publication 3-05, Washington, D.C., July 16, 2014.

———, *Department of Defense Dictionary of Military and Associated Terms*, Joint Publication 1-02, Washington, D.C., November 8, 2010, as amended through October 15, 2015.

Valentino, Benjamin, Paul Huth, and Dylan Balch-Lindsay, "'Draining the Sea': Mass Killing and Guerrilla Warfare," *International Organization,* Vol. 58, No. 2, Spring 2004, pp. 375–407.

Vandenbroucke, Lucien S., *Perilous Options: Special Operations as an Instrument of U.S. Foreign Policy*, New York: Oxford University Press, 1993.

Watts, Stephen, Caroline Baxter, Molly Dunigan, and Christopher Rizzi, *The Uses and Limits of Small-Scale Military Interventions*, Santa Monica, Calif.: RAND Corporation, MG-1226-RC, 2012. As of November 20, 2015:
http://www.rand.org/pubs/monographs/MG1226.html

Weiner, Tim, *Legacy of Ashes*, New York: Doubleday, 2007.

Weinstein, Jeremy M., *Inside Rebellion: The Politics of Insurgent Violence*, New York: Cambridge University Press, 2007.

Wells, Kevin, "8 Years of Combat FID: A Retrospective on SF in Iraq," *Special Warfare*, Vol. 25, No. 1, January–March 2012.

Witte, Griff, "After Russian Moves in Ukraine, Eastern Europe Shudders, NATO to Increase Presence," *Washington Post*, April 18, 2014.

Woodward, Bob, *Obama's Wars*, New York: Simon and Schuster, 2010.